9

THIS BOOK SHOULD BE RETURNED ON OR BEFORE THE LATEST
DATE SHOWN TO THE LIBRARY FROM WHICH IT WAS BORROWED

AUTHOR	CLASS
TAYLOR, A.	E02

TITLE
20th century blackburn

—20th Century—
BLACKBURN

by
Andrew Taylor

Wharncliffe Books

First Published in 2000 by
Wharncliffe Books
an imprint of
Pen and Sword Books Limited,
47 Church Street, Barnsley,
South Yorkshire. S70 2AS

*For up-to-date information on other titles produced under the
Wharncliffe imprint, please telephone or write to:*

    Wharncliffe Books
    FREEPOST
    47 Church Street   08342385
    Barnsley
    South Yorkshire S70 2BR
    Telephone (24 hours): 01226 - 734555

ISBN: 1-871647-89-4

A CIP catalogue record of this book is available from the
British Library

Cover illustration: Courtesy of Blackburn Libraries

Printed in Great Britain by
Redwood Books, Trowbridge, Wiltshire

Smith, Wilbur

A sparrow falls REISSUE

Macmillan   0 333 90217 3   Price: **£17.99**

600p: **24 cm**

Mark Anders returns from World War I to his native South Africa to find his grandfather has been murdered and his land confiscated. General Sean Courtney regards Mark as a son yet it is his own son who is implicated in the crime.

DOUBLE-COVER LIBRARY EDITION

CONTENTS

INTRODUCTION

Never before in the history of mankind has there been an epoch like the twentieth century. A hundred years ago, the whole world awaited the coming of this new age with eager anticipation and hopes for a better life to come.

The closing years of the nineteenth century had laid the foundations upon which some of the most profound developments of the twentieth century would be built, such as electricity, the telephone, the gramophone, the internal combustion engine and moving pictures.

During the first few years of the twentieth century, progress was moving at an ever accelerating pace, so much so that the first years of the decade saw more far reaching advances, than in any previous period of human history.

There was the first manned flight by the Wright brothers, the transmission of the first trans-Atlantic radio waves and the development of the submarine, which were all to have a profound effect on life in the twentieth century. These opening decades also witnessed the horror of war and the euphoria of peace, celebrations and distress, slumps and booms in trade, demonstrations and despair, heatwaves and cold snaps, flooding and drought, all elements which would shape the twentieth century.

Immediately following the stability of the late nineteenth century, came the death of Queen Victoria in 1901, which caused a tidal wave of instability, the effects of which would be felt through many of the coming decades. Then came the Great War, followed by the hollow carefree days of the twenties and the great stock market crash which preceded the Great Depression of the thirties and then the Second World War. The late forties brought a period of recovery, while in the fifties people "never had it so good". During the sixties and seventies came much change and a great upheaval, shaping the decades which followed. The eighties became an era of uncertainty followed by the nineties, a period which for the main part became a time of preparation for the new millennium.

But how did all of this affect Blackburn?

Many of today's history books discuss the twentieth century from an objective point of view, without specific reference to anywhere in particular. *20th Century Blackburn* however, is the subjective approach.

This is a book about Blackburn and its people during the twentieth century. Here those great national and international events are placed against a local background, showing trends and fashions, innovations and developments, policies and ideas and how these affected life in twentieth century Blackburn and the impact those events had on the town and its people.

ACKNOWLEDGEMENTS

I would like to thank all those who have assisted me in this project. To the staff in the Reference Department at Blackburn Central Library for their help in providing the relevant information sources and their patience when faced with my requests for more. In particular to Ian Sutton, Reference Librarian for his assistance, ongoing enthusiasm and help in sourcing the many photographs used and also to Diane Rushton, Local Studies Librarian, for checking copyrights and also in finding the cover illustration while the library was in a state of turmoil, as it underwent extensive building work. I would like to thank my aunt, Margaret McIntyre, for putting me on the right path to having this work published and also to Susan Halstead at the Lancashire Library Headquarters in Preston, for such valuable advice and help in locating a publisher.

I would like to thank also, Rita and Rajesh Chauhan for their help in transferring the information to a publishing compatible format and my 'personal photographer', Tim Fernandez, for the superb shots for the final chapter.

Finally, I would like to thank my Mum and Dad for their many recollections of those bygone days, making the pin-pointing of specific events easy as a result and for telling all that they came into contact with about this project and to my family, my many relations, my former work colleagues and friends both for never being surprised that I would write a book and for spurring me on by persistently asking me "When's the book coming out"?

DEDICATION

In memory of my Grandparents:
Thomas and Edith Taylor.
Harry and Pancretia Mabel Marsden.
Who witnessed the beginning of this great century.

1. SETTING THE SCENE - BLACKBURN TO AUGUST 1914.

ANY PERIOD OF TRANSITION is invariably anticipated with mixed emotions: feelings of hope and optimism, of uncertainty and apprehension and also feelings of sadness at leaving a particular era behind. As we draw ever-closer to the twenty-first century and the next millennium, these times in which we now live, generate those same emotions and although this is a time to look forward, it has also become a time to look back and reflect on the century; of people and events, long gone, almost as a means of reassurance, instinctively

Beginnings and endings - St Mary's Church, Blackburn Cathedral, March 2000. A hundred years ago, the bells of Blackburn's Parish Church, heralded the arrival of the twentieth century. Those same bells of what in this century was to become Blackburn Cathedral, signalled the end of 1999 and rang in the year 2000. Built in 1826 to replace an earlier church. The Parish was established in AD596 by Saxon settlers 404 years before the start of the second millennium. Six of the bells of the Cathedral were cast in 1737 and are said to have been cast from even older bells. *Photo Tim Fernandez.*

turning away from the next age to come, as though it is necessary to look back at the past one last time, before it is possible to move towards the next epoch which awaits. Many of the older people of today reminisce about those old days, not so much remembering specific events but on life the way it used to be when life moved at a slower pace, a world so far away from life in 1990's Blackburn. No doubt a hundred years ago the people of Blackburn experienced these emotions in much the same way as they awaited the coming of a new century.

The dawning of the twentieth century in Blackburn was awaited amidst contrasting scenes of celebration and solemnity. Crowds of people gathered in all parts, the town as busy as daytime in the hour before midnight of 31 December 1900, some congregating on the streets wishing one another well for the coming century, others filling the town's churches and chapels, attending special services to commemorate the event. As the clock of the Parish Church struck twelve midnight, the bells were rung at churches throughout Blackburn. Simultaneously, mill whistles were blown, the corporation gun sounded and rockets were fired. In the town's

Novia Scotia locks. The Leeds-Liverpool canal arrived in the town in 1816, providing a link with the port of Liverpool and an overseas market. As the cotton industry developed in the town, many mills were built on the banks of the canal to minimise transport costs.
Photo courtesy of Blackburn Library.

churches the transition from old to new was effected as worshippers were engaged in silent prayer. For better or worse, the twentieth century had arrived. The century ushered out by these celebrations, had witnessed growth unparalleled to any period gone before, a century which saw Blackburn develop from a small, relatively insignificant community, with its two cotton spinning mills, into the recognised weaving capital of the world, with its abundance of mill chimneys, standing like sentinels, guarding the mills, the town and the livelihood of the folk who lay below, dependent on cotton for survival; responsible for the blanket of smog which lingered above the town at all times, apart from the annual wakes weeks when mills closed. 'You can taste the grit from the smoke', they used to say and a change in wind direction from the prevalent west to east would blacken washing hung on lines in those districts to the west of town, but apart from the washer-women, noone really cared, since Blackburn's bread hung by Blackburn thread. There was a strong sense of optimism for the textiles industry at this time, despite the warnings in 1890, from the town's Chamber of Commerce of the dangers of 'only having one string to their bow in Blackburn', but the industry which had shaped the town so profoundly at the turn of the century, was still expanding.

Only a hundred and fifty years before the start of this most progressive of centuries, a very different place would have been encountered which had lain virtually untouched, tucked away in a pocket created by folds in the western-most vestiges of the West Pennine Moors. From the coastal plains of West Lancashire, the trek to the small community of Blackburn was a difficult one, the traveller having to negotiate marsh and moorland and muddy trails little more than cattle tracks and sheep trails; being beaten by heavy rainfall, with low cloud and mist on surrounding hills, creating a very damp environment. Having little strategic value, Roman, Dane, Celt and Norman passed by and onto places of more strategic importance, where the land was flatter and the soils richer and the terrain generally more inviting. The first known travellers who came by the area were the Romans, who's road between camps at Manchester and Ribchester, crossed the River Blakewater at the 'safe ford' - the area which came to be known as Salford, where eventually roads from Whalley, Burnley, Preston, Accrington, Bolton and Manchester converged. It was near to this crossing point, that the settlement of Blackburn began to grow and by the year AD596, Saxon settlers had built the first parish church, dedicated to St Mary, the same church mentioned in the Domesday Survey of 1086 stating: 'King Edward held Blachebourne', the whole of the area of the Blackburn Hundred being granted to Norman chief and attendant Ilbert de Lacy, the first Baron of Clitheroe by William the Conqueror.

From these beginnings, this small settlement began to grow, the original Saxon church being rebuilt during the reign of Edward III (1327-1377), being replaced by the present structure in 1826. Economically, the town developed into a regional centre and was known during the reign of Elizabeth I (1558-1603) as a market town, serving the surrounding communities, held at the junction of Darwen Street and Church Street where the Market Cross stood. The market days were Monday and Saturday with annual fairs being held on Blakey Moor each Easter Monday, 11th and 12th of May and the 17th October, for those goods and produce otherwise unobtainable outside of the region. During this same period, the Queen was petitioned, giving sanction in 1567 for the establishment of a grammar school for 'the education, management and instruction of children and youths in grammar, with 50 of the more discreet and honest inhabitants chosen to be governors of the school'.

Having little contact with the outside world, Blackburn unwittingly became involved in the English Civil War (1642-1648), when fighting broke out along Darwen Street, the Parliamentarians ambushing Royalist troops, resting in the town, the market cross being caught in the crossfire and truncated, remaining that way until its eventual removal in the nineteenth century. Prince Rupert of Hesse marched through, en-route for Yorkshire, but this was to be the town's only involvement in the Civil War. Since Blackburn remained uncommitted to either side, life resumed to the way it had been for the previous centuries, but all was to change once the impetus was provided for the industrialisation of Britain, the inhospitable climate proving to be perfect for the spinning and weaving of delicate cotton fibres for which the town was to become known throughout the world.

Owing to the poor quality of farmland in the area, peasant farmers had traditionally looked to textile production as a means of supplementing their income firstly producing woollens followed by the production of linens. The introduction of cotton in Blackburn can be traced back as far as 1650 at a time when Blackburn was emerging as the centre for the manufacture of fustian, a cloth composed of a flax weft and a cotton warp, and was known for the weaving of the Blackburn Check, superseded in the eighteenth century by the plainer fustian cloth, the Blackburn Grey. Progress in the industry was slow, that is until 1764, when James Hargreaves of

The Market Hall on Market day with stalls lining, King William Street.
Photo courtesy of Blackburn Library.

Stanhill, near Oswaldtwistle invented the 'spinning jenny', providing the catalyst which led to the development of Richard Arkwright's 'waterframe' and later, Samuel Crompton's 'mule', spinning machines which had the ability to overcome the inadequacy of existing spinning wheels and produce a strong cotton weft enabling the production of the all-cotton cloth - calico. The advent of steam-power revolutionised the industry still further, since power could be applied to both waterframe and mule and by 1775, factories for the spinning of yarn began to appear in Blackburn though the town retained its rustic character as weaving remained largely a domestic trade due to the practical problem of developing a powerloom able to weave the fine cotton cloths that were being woven at that time on the traditional handloom.

From this day forward, the population of the town began to increase at an alarming rate, rising from 8,000 in 1780 to 11,980 by the start of the nineteenth century, a trend which was repeated throughout this century, as more and more people were brought to the town in search of employment, averaging a rate over the whole of the nineteenth century of about 10,000 per decade. In order to cope with this huge influx, many houses were built, squeezed into a relatively small area, lacking adequate sanitation, with several households having to share a single tap and one WC and not unexpectedly, the occurrence of infectious diseases in the town was not uncommon, the town's unenviably high mortality rate being exceeded only by the City of Liverpool, until the installation of

Salford Bridge, the town's historic centre, where the Roman road, between camps in Manchester and Ribchester, crossed the River Blakewater. *Photo courtesy of Blackburn Library.*

improved drains which halved the rate at a stroke.

Once cut off from the outside world, the growth of the cotton trade coupled with improved communications, meant that Blackburn was no longer the isolated community, little known outside the immediate area. A scheme of road improvements was undertaken in the early part of the nineteenth century and by 1816, communications were improved still further with the arrival of the Leeds-Liverpool Canal, linking the Blackburn cotton industry with an overseas market, via the Port of Liverpool. The railway arrived in 1846, by which time the improved powerloom had been perfected by James Bullough and William Kenworthy of Brookhouse Mill, having the ability to weave the finest of cotton cloths. As a result, mills for the weaving of cotton cloth began to appear which, displaced a long established cottage industry. In 1851, Queen Victoria granted Blackburn the Charter of Incorporation, creating the Borough of Blackburn and there followed greater town planning and civic improvements. The laying of the Corporation Park in 1853, the Town Hall of 1856, the Cotton Exchange of 1863, the Free Library and Museum of 1862, the elegant Thwaites's shopping Arcade of 1883 and the Technical College built during 1888, joined the Market Hall of 1848 and its adjoining market square as notable developments at

that time. By the later decades of the nineteenth century, the Borough set about a scheme of improvements, tackling a programme of slum clearance, providing larger, better quality rows of terraced houses, each provided with running water and WC. At the centre of town, the River Blakewater was culverted, and at Salford, the original hump-backed bridge, a notorious bottleneck, even in the days of horse-drawn vehicles, was removed and the area levelled and widened. A new railway station was constructed, to alleviate congestion there, as more rail-routes were provided to and from Blackburn, and the area in front of the station, once a marshy wasteland, was drained and transformed into the Boulevard, providing a terminus for the horse-drawn, steam and later electric trams which appeared during 1899. By the final year of the nineteenth century, there existed, 129 cotton mills in Blackburn, employing 41,400 people, a figure representing 38% of the town's total population which was estimated as being around the 129,000 mark as the century was drawing to a close.

And so after our sojourn into the depths of time, we arrive back at the point at which the twentieth century was born, into an atmosphere of hope and of anticipation of better opportunities, improved conditions and times of greater security and prosperity, with brass bands playing throughout the borough as the first light of this new century dawned in celebration of the coming of this new age. For the first couple of years, life in Blackburn like the rest of the country remained little altered being involved in events of a national flavour. The death of Queen Victoria, just three weeks into this century, plunged the town and nation into a state of mourning, with memorial services being held at churches and chapels throughout Blackburn on the day of the state funeral. Following a civic service at the Parish Church, the council held a special meeting, setting up a public subscription to finance a scheme to construct a memorial in honour of the 'glorious and beneficial' reign of the late Queen. In contrast, there was celebration during May 1902 at the ending of the Boer War, sending the whole town into a state of euphoria. It was during this most protracted of colonial skirmishes that James Pitt became the first man from Blackburn to be awarded the Victoria Cross, given to him for his single-handed defence of a Caesar's Camp, a remote, yet strategic out-post, during the siege of Ladysmith. A month after the ending of the war, came the intended coronation of King Edward VII and Queen Alexandra, and even the postponement of the event due to the king having to undergo emergency surgery for appendicitis did not halt proceedings in Blackburn, the street-parties, fireworks displays and the illumination of the town hall going ahead as planned. Further celebrations two months later were held in honour of the rearranged coronation, marking the beginning of a new epoch, the Edwardian age, an era associated with 'nostalgia and gaiety', but where divides between rich and poor remained just as wide. For cotton workers however, there was a glimmer of hope on the horizon during 1902, when members of the weaving association, voted overwhelmingly to finish work at 12:00 noon on Saturdays, enabling weavers to enjoy a little more leisure time.

In those so called, 'good old days' however, times were still hard for many, the average working man still working long hours. Music Hall provided a release from the toils of the working week and in those golden days of variety, Blackburn's three variety theatres, the Princes, the Palace and the Lyceum, presented many of the music hall greats. Dan Leno, Wal Pink, Walford Bodie, Vesta Tilley with the legendary 'Burlington Bertie' routine, Lafeyette, Rishton's, Choo Lin

Su, George Formby Senior, Vesta Victoria, Lottie Collins, with her rumbustuous rendition of the song 'Ta-ra-ra-boom-dye-aye', all played Blackburn's music halls, in addition to a deluge of conjurers, illusionists, acrobats, many whose names have been lost in the passage of time, but nevertheless made a valuable contribution to the town's popular entertainment of that golden age. There was much excitement, when Houdini appeared at the Palace Theatre of Variety on the Boulevard. After asking for a volunteer, Blackburn based crime writer, W Hope Hodgson was chosen, who using his knowledge of muscle structures, bound Houdini so well, that it took the great escapologist over two hours to escape, by means judged by an unbiased on-looker, as unsatisfactory. Needless to say, a riot broke out in the highly charged audience, resulting in the Police being called in asking Hodgson to leave and evacuating the house for fear it might be wrecked.

Another variety house, Ohmy's Circus, stood at the corner of Mill Lane and Mincing Lane, where the New Central Hall now stands. Housed in a wooden building, the circus presented acts from around the world, including some who claimed to have performed at the famous 'Barnum and Bailey' circus in the United States, and not forgetting, the 'Great Ohmy' himself - trapeze artist Joe Smith from Rochdale, whom, it is claimed, was so daring on the flying trapeze, that his feats made the audience gasp in horror and cry out as one, 'Oh my!'. Legendary Blackburn Acrobat, Jack Higgins leaped over the heads of twenty horses at the circus and itinerant street performer, Richard Thompson, alias, 'Strong Dick' made his first public appearance there, accepting a wager to lift an iron bar of 260lbs, receiving the princely sum of five shillings (25p), for accomplishing the challenge. The circus also became a venue for public meetings and it was there in 1901, the Blackburn Labour Party adopted Philip Snowden as their prospective parliamentary candidate for Blackburn.

The town's Theatre Royal, with its characteristic semi-circular frontage stood on Ainsworth Street, providing a diverse programme of entertainment to suit most tastes, ranging from repertory, opera, and choral to variety under the auspices of Walter De Frece, husband of Vesta Tilley. Many of the country's distinguished actors strode the boards at this venerable old theatre, the successor of the 'New Theatre', Blackburn's first theatre established in 1787, replaced in 1818 by the first Theatre Royal, which was rebuilt during 1867. The leading tour companies regularly visited and it was here in 1903, that a young actor, Charlie Chaplin, made an early career appearance, playing the part of Billy the page boy in a production of Sherlock Holmes, following in the footsteps of Mrs Dorothea Jordan, The Kendals, the Great Macready, Wilson Barrett, Lillie Langtree, Sir Henry Irving and the virtuoso Italian violinist, Niccolo Paganini.

In contrast there was also the town's annual fair, which rolled into the town each Easter, taking residence on the market square its home since moving from Blakey Moor in 1852. Since the mid-nineteenth century the importance of the fair as a trading centre had diminished as a result of transport improvements, wares once difficult to obtain, being easily acquired as a result of these improvements. The once vital trading element however, still existed in the form of the pot fair, but the greatest emphasis at the turn of the century was on the fun side becoming the blight of authorities and industrialists alike who had on several times attempted to banish the fair from the town, believing this proto-industrial event to have no place in industrialised Blackburn. From 1865 however, this lively, colourful spectacle had undergone its own industrial revolution, the shows once the mainstays of the event being displaced from the centre ground by the latest in ambulatory attractions powered by steam; rides such as the gallopers, the steam yachts, scenic railways with their huge carved dragons, the cakewalk, Helter Skelter and the latest, the eccentric Razzle Dazzle. Ornate, carved pipe-organs, belted out the popular tunes of the day as showmen shouted out 'roll up, roll up!' to tempt the inquisitive into the booths around the margins of the fair, to see the latest in freak shows: the fat lady, the five-legged sheep, the bearded lady, the India rubber man all there creating an atmosphere unique to the fair. Bioscope shows were in attendance at the fair during the earliest years of the century, giving many people of Blackburn, their first opportunity to experience the wonder of moving pictures.

But for Blackburn, it most definitely wasn't all beer and skittles in this first period of the twentieth century, especially in 1904, when disaster struck and the cotton industry was hit by a disastrous slump, reminding industrialists of the Chamber of Commerce's ominous message and dismissing the belief that slumps in the cotton trade would be left behind as a feature of the nineteenth century were wrong and with it, the bitter realisation that changes for the better would not come about in a matter of a few years. Though there were other industries in Blackburn, engineering, brewing and building being three of the other main ones, the problem was that these too were dependent on the state of the cotton trade, so slumps like the one which struck the textile industry in 1904, cut deep into

Church Street from its junction with Darwen Street, with Thwaites's Arcade on the left. Note the two weavers on the right with shawls.

Photo courtesy of Blackburn Library.

Blackburn's economy. With thousands unemployed in the town, the need for drastic action was urgently required. A public meeting held at the town hall to address the problem, passed a resolution urging the Government to give 'immediate and practical' assistance to the efforts of the Cotton Growers Association, to increase supplies of cotton in the Empire and to minimalise the effects of this slump by getting the mills of Blackburn back to full production.

Things looked better for the industry in 1905, when the Livesey Mill Building Company formed to build a weaving mill on land near the canal at Mill Hill. Leased to the Pioneer Mill Company, this mill opened later that year, the first new weaving mill to open in the twentieth century and the first of five weaving mills opened during that year. But the seemingly blinkered view of those Blackburn industrialists failed to see that expanding the town's cotton trade just added to the problems of distress brought about by slumps in the trade. Instead of introducing more of the same they should have been looking at ways of bringing new industries to the town, which were not dependent on the state of the cotton trade. Yet whilst cotton boomed and slumps were regarded as a tiresome and temporary setback by mill owners, such a notion to try and diversify trade in Blackburn fell aside.

By the late summer of 1905, the memorial to Queen Victoria was nearing completion. Australian sculptor, Bertram Mackennal, protégé of opera singer, Nellie Melba, had been commissioned to produce a statue of the late Queen by the Victoria Memorial Committee, established at the Queen's death in January 1901. Within four years £10,500 had been raised by public subscription and by the autumn of 1905, the statue had been positioned in a prominent site overlooking the Boulevard, ready for public viewing. The unveiling ceremony took place on 30 September, performed by the late Queen's fourth daughter, Princess Louise, Duchess of Argyll, accompanied by the usual pomp present on these occasions. Thousands of people given the day off work, specially for the occasion, witnessed the Princess tug a cord, revealing the splendid statue of Queen Victoria in full regalia, sculpted out of white Sicilian Marble and mounted on a grey granite plinth, the event marked by flags and bunting, decorating the streets of Blackburn. Following speeches, the Royal Party proceeded in carriages, escorted by the Duke of Lancaster's Own Imperial Yeomanry, to a civic reception at the town hall, along a route lined with thousands more people. The celebrations carried on into the evening with a promenade concert at Corporation Park, whilst Queen's Park was illuminated with oriental lanterns. A military band played there before a grand fireworks display brought proceedings in honour of the Royal visit to a close.

As the century entered its sixth year, the drive for better health, better education, emancipation and improved conditions, denied to so many was beginning to accelerate. Calls for reform were gaining strength as a result of the industrial classes swelling beneath the upper classes, causing a destabilising factor. Times-were-a-changing as the working man became more politically aware and began to question the established order where rigid social codes determined relations between people of different rank and sex. The General Election of that year saw Philip Snowden, become Blackburn's first Labour Member of Parliament, occupying the seat vacated by the retirement of mill-owner and Conservative MP, William Coddington; one of twenty-six labour MP's elected to Parliament for the first time since the birth of the Labour movement just six years earlier. Christobel Pankhurst, visited Blackburn on 10 March that same year, addressing two meetings in the town. From a platform on the Market Square, she spoke on the matter of providing meals for school children, correlating the lack of proper nourishment with crime arguing that one good meal a day could 'considerably cut the numbers of inmates in these institutions'.

At a second meeting later that same day at the Independent Labour Club, Miss Pankhurst lectured on her specialist subject, questioning Britain's electoral system, which denied women the right to vote, a crusade for which she herself, her mother Emmeline and sisters Sylvia and Adela, campaigned tirelessly. Calling on the assembled members, she asked them 'to reconsider and give their consent to the issue of women's right to vote'. As it became obvious the Liberal Government was not going to give women the vote, the Women's Suffragette movement resorted to more radical and violent tactics and began to gain support from the town's women as the group became more active. During a particularly riotous demonstration outside the Houses of Parliament, Blackburn woman, Teresa Billington was one of eleven suffragettes arrested and subsequently imprisoned for her part in the incident which led to a particularly stormy encounter with Police. Hailed as great heroines, Miss Billington and the other gaoled suffragettes were honoured at a celebratory luncheon at London's Savoy Hotel following their release. Louisa Entwistle another leading suffragette from Blackburn, who was one of 75 women, imprisoned after a demonstration in London during March 1907, but undeterred by such penalties, these spirited ladies continued with their

The Cotton Exchange, King William Street pictured in 1909, which a year earlier, had become the town centre's first cinema which showed films at regular nightly performances. The view down King William Street to Sudell Cross has changed little in a hundred years. *Photo courtesy of Blackburn Library.*

campaigning, challenging the electoral system and calling for change. In Blackburn, not surprisingly, there was opposition to the Suffragette movement and the Anti-women's Suffrage League was established in Blackburn by one Fred Hargreaves, a well known liberal of those times, who claimed out of 363 women he had spoken to, only thirteen were interested in gaining the vote. Yet despite this stand, people power was gaining in strength nation-wide, becoming a real threat to the established order based on privilege and obedience.

There was encouraging news for the people of Blackburn during 1907, following the publication of a report, which found there to be a fall in the town's infant mortality rate, a figure which had remained consistently high ever since the industrialisation of the town. In this year, General Booth, leader of the Salvation Army visited Blackburn, the new General Post Office on Darwen Street opened, replacing the existing one in Lord Street and the Fountains and Fernhurst Weaving Mills went into production, yet in spite of these further expansions in the weaving trade, the industry was hit once again by a devastating slump in trade the following year, rendering a quarter of the town's looms idle with 43 mills stopped entirely. With little organised welfare available to help those without work, soup kitchens were set up throughout the borough and half of those who had been laid off had need to turn to the distress committee for help. On the development front, 1908 saw the foundation stone of the YMCA in Limbrick laid by Lord Kinnaird, President of the National Council for the YMCA and visitors to Blackburn in this year of gloom included Labour Party Chairman, James Keir Hardie and his deputy, Ramsey MacDonald, who both addressed meetings at the town's Prince's Theatre.

By this time, new forms of entertainment were beginning to appear including the establishment of permanent cinema which by 1908, had been established at the Victoria Hall, Eanam Bridge and at the Exchange Hall in King William Street. The advent of moving pictures in 1895 had seen Blackburn at the forefront of developments in this area. Just ten months after the first recognised moving picture show in Paris, they were exhibited at the Lyceum Theatre in Market Street Lane. Realising the potential, Blackburn film enthusiasts, Sagar J Mitchell and James Kenyon, began producing films to supply fairground bioscope shows, becoming the only film-making company of any note in Edwardian Lancashire. Their many achievements include the filming of mock Boer War battles on moors surrounding the town, complete with explosions, created by scratching star shapes on individual frames of film, appearing as flashes once the film was in motion and also creating an effect using cinematographic techniques for music hall star, Perci Honri, whereby the moon complete with face, projected onto a back-cloth at the Palace Theatre, winced and frowned as Honri sang. Despite their contribution to the early days of cinema, Mitchell and Kenyon's film-making days came to an unfortunate end, just as cinema was taking off in a big way, when whilst filming on the North Pier at Blackpool a huge wave washed their film making equipment away.

As the growth in the popularity of moving pictures continued, two more cinemas opened in Blackburn during 1909, at a time when roller-skating was enjoying a revival. In response to the re-emergence of this craze up and down the country and believing it to be big business, three rinks were built in the town. First to open was the Blackburn Rink, built on the site of the former Ohmy's Circus, but the anticipated popularity was somewhat over estimated as the rink was hastily reconstructed into a picture house just nine months after first opening. The following year saw the opening of the Star Picture Palace, Little Harwood and the Empire Electric Theatre, Ewood, whilst a second roller skating rink, the Olympia on St Peter Street, switched to moving pictures exhibition in 1911, becoming the eighth cinema to open in Blackburn in a little over three years, posing a threat to the town's established theatres and music halls whose popularity from this point in time was beginning to wane a little in the face of this new and rapidly increasing form of popular entertainment.

As this first decade of the twentieth century was drawing to a close, there was a significant albeit small fall in the number of inmates at the Union Workhouse. Built by inmates during the devastating cotton famine of 1864, to replace an earlier building, this formidable institution, menacingly overlooked the town from the bleak, windswept plateau of Whinney Heights, providing accommodation to paupers, the aged, orphans, vagrants, the unemployed, the homeless and others who were unable to support themselves, banished out of sight of the 'betters' of society, who believed that poverty was self-imposed, but who's notion of diligence and hard work providing adequate means and prosperity, overlooked the problems of unemployment caused by economic slumps and infectious diseases which starved people of their dignity, their dependants and their means. From time to time, rumours regarding conditions at the workhouse, descended onto a town shocked by tales of maggot-infested beds and buildings over-run with vermin.

There were murmurs of cruelty inflicted on both staff and inmates and tales of badly undernourished children having to work in coal pits for long hours.

It was the Liberal Government between 1909 and 1911, which first began to tackle the problems of poverty, introducing reforms, to enable these people to escape the clutches of the workhouse. The first of these reforms, the Old Age Pensions Act came into force in 1909, but despite the horrors associated with life at the Blackburn workhouse, only 14 out of the 150 inmates eligible, made a claim for the weekly pension of five shillings (25p), the rest prepared to stay where they were. The first Labour Exchange opened in Blackburn in 1910, with over a hundred men registering in its first day, followed by the introduction of the National Insurance Act, enabling certain workers to qualify for benefits at times of sickness and unemployment, a particularly welcome measure in Blackburn, with its cotton industry reliant on the whims of an erratic trade cycle - an unfavourable turn leaving thousands in the town without work or any source of financial support prior to the introduction of this act. By 1912, these and a number of smaller acts introduced, provided people with the opportunity to escape forever the pull of the workhouse, as inmate numbers began to fall marking the beginning of the end of the workhouse.

The opening of the new Police Station and Sessions House on Northgate, the unveiling of the statue in Limbrick in memory of William Henry Hornby, the Borough's first mayor, by his son, Blackburn's Conservative MP, Sir Harry Hornby and the opening of the reconstructed County Court, all took place in the eventful year of 1912 in which industry and transport were badly affected as a result of a coal dispute. Two men from the town, engineer Jonathan Shepherd and steward Thomas Teuton, were amongst the 1,513 people who perished in the freezing waters of the Atlantic when the Titanic went down but the big news in Blackburn came in the late spring of 1912 when Blackburn Rovers achieved their first Football League Championship. Formed in 1875, the club had been founder members of the Football League in 1888, but despite enjoying immense success in the FA Cup; being the first non-public school team to reach the FA Cup final in 1882, and then two years later winning the trophy for the first of their five FA Cup successes between 1884 and 1891, the League Championship had eluded them in 23 attempts. Their eventual success continued, ending what was hailed as their greatest season to date by clinching victory in the Charity Shield.

BLACKBURN ROVER'S FOOT BALL TEAM 1908,,9, N⁰ 91.

Blackburn Rovers 1908-9. The first decade of the twentieth century saw the Rovers gradually improve on their positions in the Football League each season. They finished 4th in 1908-09 season, one place better in the following season, before becoming League Champions in both the 1911-12 and 1913-14 seasons. *Photo courtesy of Blackburn Library.*

It was during the following year when Blackburn was one of the Lancashire town's honoured by a visit from King George V and Queen Mary who were embarking on a week-long tour of the county. Following a tour of Roe Lee Mill, the king and queen moved onto the town centre to a specially constructed platform outside the town hall where the King pushed a button which sent an electrical current down a cable, activating a crane out of sight in Northgate, which lowered the foundation stone of the new public halls into place. Other visitors during 1913, included the distinguished British Composer, Gustav Von Holst and the Irish dramatist, George Bernard Shaw. The Malvern and Eclipse Mills began production as suffragettes whose failure to secure the vote, launched a campaign of arson, targeting recognised bastions of male domination. Two of the town's mills were struck by mysterious fires, whilst a blatant attempt by the suffragettes to burn down the grandstand at Ewood Park failed when smoke was observed coming from the structure. The

Visit of King George V and Queen Mary, to lay the foundation stone of the new public halls in Northgate. They are pictured here on the specially constructed platform outside the main entrance of the town hall. *Photo courtesy of Blackburn Library.*

following year, the town was rudely awakened one Sunday evening by the sound of the ornamental Russians canons in Corporation Park, being primed and fired by suffragettes with a note being found close by with the message 'Wake up Blackburn!' written on it, the suffragettes certainly making themselves heard throughout the borough!

In what was to become the final year of peace, before Europe was torn apart by war, Blackburn Rovers won a second League Championship, shortly before European events threw the world into utter chaos. Life in Blackburn up to the summer of 1914, carried on pretty much as normal, with a ballot voting in favour of moving the annual Blackburn Holidays wakes weeks from the first week in August to the third week in July and abolishing the annual week's holiday at Whitsuntide in favour of the third week in September. Plans to construct parks at Roe Lee and off Aqueduct Road, Ewood, were approved, the town's population was still expanding, peaking at almost 140,000, the crown of king cotton sparkled brilliantly, the foundations being laid for the Longshaw Mill as the cotton trade expanded still further, and Mr and Mrs R A Yerburgh of Woodfold Hall, Mellor were visiting friends at Bad Nachaim in Germany, which would not have been of any real consequence had it not been for events in Europe, leaving the Yerburghs stranded in what was to become enemy territory. The cessation of work for the annual Blackburn Holidays at the beginning of August 1914, occurred at a time of a particularly hot spell of weather, in the midst of the uneasy European situation. The assassination of the heir to the Austrian throne by a Serbian nationalist in the Austro-Hungarian controlled city of Sarajevo, prompted the Austro-Hungarians to declare war on Serbia. A complex web of treaties assuring assistance to countries on opposing sides of the conflict began to tighten, Germany on the side of Austria-Hungary, Russia and France on the Serbian side. On 3 August, the German Army marched into neutral Belgium. As a matter of honour and in response to an unproved attack on a neutral country, Great Britain and its nation was drawn into this European conflict, rapidly escalating into the Great War.

And so all the hopes, the ideas for a better world and the struggles for reform and equality that were present at the start of this century disintegrated as war loomed. For the people of Blackburn it had been a period of swings and roundabouts. The first fourteen years of this century saw more far reaching advances than had ever been witnessed in any period gone before and those changes which had taken place laid the foundations for even more sweeping reforms to be built upon. But these years had also witnessed unfavourable effects of the slumps in the cotton trade and the despair they caused. For the time being however, any plans for the future were put on hold and the era which began with celebrations of stability, ended with instability and total chaos becoming the last period of peace before Europe was torn apart by war. The Victorian sunset which had warmed the Edwardian years, had finally set as the long and bitter winter of the Great War dawned and for Blackburn like so many other places, life would never be quite the same again.

EVENTS - 1900-August 1914

1900
• Hundreds congregate in all parts of Blackburn to await the arrival of the twentieth century, (31 Dec).

1901
• The Parish Church rings in the twentieth century, (1 Jan).
• Borough decides to light tram routes.
• Death of Queen Victoria, (22 Jan)
• Public Subscription set up to raise £10,000 to build monument in honour of the late Queen.
• Shareholders of the Blackburn Cotton Exchange draw their last dividends and are discharged as last duty.
• Victoria Cross conferred on Blackburn Soldier, James Pitt.
• Heavy flooding in the Salford area, worst for 36 years.
• Blackburn Socialists adopt Philip Snowden as prospective parliamentary candidate.
• Opening of the new St Albans RC Church
• Last steam powered tram withdrawn from service.
• Guardians of Blackburn Workhouse vote against the abolition of the grinding of corn by inmates.
• Electrification of the Cemetery and Accrington Road tram routes.
• Population of Blackburn 129,216.

1902
• Textile Workers Act comes into force.
• Telephone company introduces party telephone lines.
• Death at Klippan, South Africa, of the Lord of the Manor of Blackburn, Major William Cecil Montague Feilden, succeeded by his younger brother Captain James Hawley Gilbert Feilden.
• The 24 car owners in Blackburn form the North East Lancashire Automobile Club.
• Celebrations mark the ending of the Boer War, (7 June).
• *Lyceum Theatre,* Market Street Lane forced to close down, due to reports of   notoriety.
• Celebrations mark the Coronation of King Edward VII, the Borough's first Freeman, (9 Aug).
• Houdini appears at the *Palace Theatre,* Boulevard.
• Market holders request the removal of the annual Easter Fair.
• Extension of Cemetery tram route to Wilpshire

1903
• David Lloyd George addresses meeting at the Exchange Hall.
• Banana Plants introduced at *Corporation Park Conservatory.*
• Charlie Chaplin appears at the *Theatre Royal.*
• Extension of tram line from Witton Stocks to *Cherry Tree.*

1904
• Meeting at town hall expresses concern at serious shortages of cotton.
• James Pitt, hero of the Boer War returns home to civic welcome.
• Report announces fall in both the town's birth and death rate.
• Foundation stone of Blackburn Orphanage laid at Wilpshire.
• Brilliant Comet seen from town.

1905
• Livesey Mill Building company formed building new weaving mill at *Mill Hill, (Pioneer Mill)*
• Blackburn Orphanage opened.
• Drought conditions cause suspension of traffic on the canal.

- Motorist fined £10 for speeding through Salford Bridge at 10 mph.
- Visit of Princess Louise to unveil statue of Queen Victoria.
- Markets Committee vote against the abolition of the annual Easter Fair.
- Unity, Grange, Hollinshead and Royal weaving mills begin production.

1906
- Philip Snowden elected as Blackburn's first Labour MP, (20 Jan).
- Visit of Christobel Pankhurst.
- Erection of grandstand at *Ewood Park* begins.
- Visit of Labour Party Chairman, J Keir Hardie.
- Blackburn suffragette, Teresa Billington, arrested outside the Houses of Parliament.
- Salisbury and Parkside mills open.

1907
- Fall in town's infant mortality rate.
- Blackburn Suffragette, Louisa Entwistle arrested in London.
- League set up in town to oppose the granting of the vote to women.
- Visit of General Booth leader of the Salvation Army.
- Blackburn's first permanent cinema opens at the Victoria Hall, Eanam.
- Adela Pankhurst and Mrs Philip Snowden address meeting about Women's Suffrage at the Lees Hall.
- General Post Office, *Darwen Street* opened.
- Fountains and *Fernhurst Mills* built.

1908
- Foundations of YMCA, Limbrick laid.
- Nightly cinema introduced at the *Exchange Hall,* King William Street.
- Open-air gramophone recitals commence at *Corporation Park.*
- Approval given to build school and swimming baths at Blakey Moor.
- Penalty imposed on householders failing to replace ash pits with galvanised dustbins.
- Engagement of Clementine Hosier, a distant relative of the Feildens of Witton Park, to Winston Churchill.
- Lively scenes at Suffragette meeting on the market place.
- First pension papers distributed to all people in the town over 70.
- 34 mills stopped due to changes in cotton industry.
- Keir Hardie and Ramsey MacDonald address meeting at the *Prince's Theatre.*

1909
- Old Age Pensions Act comes into force, (1 Jan).
- *Theatre Royal* reopens as *Royal Hippodrome* after refurbishment.
- Extensions to the Infirmary opened.
- Opening of *Harrison's Gymnasium.*
- The *Blackburn, Olympia* and *Witton* Roller Skating Rinks open.
- Opening of the *Alexandra* and *Kings Picture Halls.*
- *Blackburn* Roller Skating Rink becomes the *Central Cinema.*

1910
- Blackburn's first Labour Exchange opens.
- *Star* and *Empire* Cinemas opened.
- Death of Edward VII, Borough's first freeman, (6 May).
- Sir Harry Hornby officially opens the YMCA.,

1911

- Introduction of the National Insurance Act, (1 Jan).
- *Blakey Moor* Higher Elementary School opens.
- National Railway strike leaves hundreds of Blackburn holiday makers stranded, (19 Aug).
- Member of staff at the *Blackburn Times,* receives UK's first aerial post.
- Harrison's Institute opened - 150 girls enrol on first day.
- Weaving working at full capacity, all available looms operating.
- Blackburn Branch of *Women's Suffrage Society* formed.
- *Olympia* Roller Skating Rink becomes a cinema.
- Establishment of Scotland Bank and Haston Lee weaving mills.

1912

- Cotton lock-out.
- Blackburn Rovers beaten 1-0 after extra time in FA Cup semi-final replay against West Bromwich Albion
- Plan to improve town centre announced.
- Curtailed rail services to and from town, due to national coal strike.
- Blackburn Rovers win their first Football League Championship.
- Titanic sinks - 2 men from Blackburn perish in the tragedy (15 Apr).
- Blackburn Rovers achieve 2-1 victory over QPR in the Charity Shield, the event being brought forward to the close of the 1911-12 season, to raise money for the *Titanic Relief Fund* (4 May).
- Bandstand erected, *Queens Park.*
- Sir Harry Hornby unveils statue of WH Hornby in Limbrick.
- Opening of Police Station and *Sessions House,* Northgate.
- Rebuilt County Court, Victoria Street, opened.
- Fall in inmates at the Blackburn *Union Workhouse.*
- Death of street entertainer, Robert Renolds, aged 88, alias *'Owd chipper'.*
- Lever, Prospect, Durbar, Newton Street, India and Didsbury Street
- Mills start up.

1913

- Cab shelter, Boulevard, built.
- Gustav Von Holst conducts Ladies Choir at concert at the Town hall.
- Visit of King George V and Queen Mary to lay foundation stone of the new public assembly halls, Northgate.
- Visit of Irish dramatist, George Bernard Shaw.
- Picture houses lose right to employ vocalists.
- Lawn tennis league is set up with teams in Blackburn, Rishton, Great Harwood, Darwen and Chorley due to increase in popularity of the sport.
- Suffragettes embark on a campaign of arson, attempting to burn down the *Nuttall* Street Stand at *Ewood Park.*
- Short-term working imposed at Blackburn's mills due to shortages of orders.
- Malvern and Eclipse Weaving Mills begin production.

1914

- Suffragettes fire ornamental canons at *Corporation Park.*
- Ballot votes on favour of moving annual Blackburn Wakes Holiday.
- Blackburn Rovers win first division league championship for a second time.
- Suffragettes disrupt and barrack meeting at the *Olympia* Picture Theatre.
- Foundations laid for Longshaw weaving mill and for the new church of *St Peter,* Mill Hill.
- Assassination of Archduke Franz Ferdinand, Sarajevo, Austria-Hungary declares war on Serbia (28 Jun).
- Closure of town's mills for the annual Blackburn Holidays (1 Aug).
- German invasion of Belgium (2 Aug).
- Great Britain declares war on Germany (4 Aug).

2. KEEPING THE HOME FIRES BURNING - AUGUST 1914-1919.

A PERIOD OF SUSPENSE FOLLOWED news of the German invasion of Belgium with crowds gathering in Blackburn, like elsewhere in the country, around newspaper offices, the first port of call for the announcement of any major news item. Thousands stood in Railway Road, awaiting news of the latest developments and despite the numbers there was little noise apart from the muffled sound of people talking, broken by one mans spurious claim that the war had broken out as he said he could hear the sound of gunfire coming from the East. But eventually at around 8.00pm on 4 August, the anticipation and suspense came to an end with the posting of the long-awaited telegram in the window of the offices of the Northern Daily Telegraph, with the message: 'Great Britain at War with Germany'.

The prospect of a showdown with the despised hun, provided an opportunity too good to miss for the people of Great Britain, the war being seen as a patriotic crusade against the Kaiser, a despotic leader of an aggressive nation. With little prompting, those who had spent the previous fourteen years rebelling against a rigid and discriminatory class system, dutifully rallied to the call of King and Empire, falling behind the upper classes who instinctively took the reins, luxuriating in the glory of successful campaigns, but distancing themselves from the many disasters and huge losses. In line with other places throughout Britain, the men of Blackburn responded nobly to the call to arms, swept along by the same euphoria that had swept the country believing the propaganda that this would be the war to end all wars and it would all be over by Christmas. Such was the response in the town, that extra staff were required at the Canterbury Street Barracks to cope with this huge influx of men willing to fight for their country. By the beginning of September 1914, the first detachment of local territorials were ready to embark on foreign duties, ceremoniously parading to the Parish Church on the night before they set off to war, depositing their regimental colours to be reclaimed once their duty had been done and peace had been restored. Hundreds turned out to see the first wave of soldiers depart and wish them luck as they set out on a journey leading to those far off places, whose names over eighty years later

The Town Hall and Market Hall, King William Street in the summer of 1914, a serene scene taken shortly before Europe was thrown into turmoil with the outbreak of the Great War. *Photo courtesy of Blackburn Library.*

Volunteers for the Athletes Volunteer Force, assemble at the Drill Hall, the former Witton Roller Skating Rink. These men would have been allocated to various regiments, the majority going to the East Lancashire Regiment. *Photo courtesy of Blackburn Library.*

conjour up mental pictures of the horrors of trench warfare, synonymous with a no-mans land, littered with craters, barbed wire, abandoned canons and tanks stuck in mud: Mons, Cambrai, The Atus, Neuve Chapelle, Verdun, The Somme, Arras, Amiens, Ypres and Passchendaele and the lands of the former Ottoman Empire - Egypt, Palestine, Mesopotamia, Salonika, Alexandria, Gallipoli and the Dardenelles, the first point of contact in the War for the Blackburn division of the East Lancashire Regiment.

Although in Blackburn, during the first few months of the war, life continued as normal as possible under the circumstances, it was down to the women of the town to show their worth and undertake tasks once the domain of men. Though in Blackburn's cotton industry, the employment of women was nothing extraordinary, it was in fields such as tram driving and working in the Police force. The Suffragette movement suspended all their activities, pledging their undivided support to the Government whilst the nation was at war, encouraging women to do all in their will to help out. As a result, women were also drafted into heavy industry, employed in the manufacture of munitions, at places like the Atlas Foundry of Clayton and Goodfellow off Audley in the hope that they could help bring the war to a swift conclusion, but as Christmas 1914 passed and 1915 dawned, there seemed little chance of this conflict ending as soon as anticipated when war broke out.

By the start of 1915, over 7,000 men from the town had enlisted though the poor health of many of the town's men was highlighted by the higher than national average 25% rejection rate. In a year which saw legislation introduced to raise the maximum age of volunteers to 40 and reduced the minimum height of recruits in order to swell ranks, the War Office introduced the notion of 'Pals Battalions' to induce whole groups of people; gangs of friends, neighbours and even factory workers to enlist together in the knowledge that they would be fighting side by side in the war zones of Europe. For most, going off to war was the first time that they had been so far away from home, so it would be reassuring for them, knowing that it would be all friends together. From the politician's point of view, such a scheme could greatly increase the number of recruits and provide a steady flow of volunteers based on a notion that if one friend joined up others would follow. A recruiting office for the Blackburn Pal's Battalion was set up in Preston New Road, with fifty men enlisting in the first few days and pictures of these Battalions appeared on the pages of the town's newspapers, soldiers proudly posing in their uniforms, eagerly awaiting departure in the belief that it was one great adventure and a chance to see a little bit of the world away from the smoky world of Blackburn. A cadet force was also formed in the town in this year and in order to extend the town's war effort still further and satisfy the never-ending demand for volunteers, recruiting drives were held throughout Blackburn with orators using all in their powers to persuade more and more of the town's men to enlist. At one rally outside the gates of Corporation Park, 5000 were present to hear Deputy Mayor, Alderman Crossley call upon the women of the town, to persuade 'sweethearts' to prove themselves, by enlisting to 'maintain the freedom and liberty they enjoyed'. Nowhere was free from the call for king and country, street corners, the market place, mills and during intervals at the town's theatres and picture houses, but what most volunteers failed to realise was their departure from Blackburn Station would be by way of a one-way ticket.

Another great maritime tragedy struck during the summer of

1915, with the torpedoing and subsequent sinking of the British passenger liner, the Lusitania, off the coast of Southern Ireland by a German U-boat. Former Blackburn woman, Mrs Alfred Duckworth was one of the survivors of this catastrophe, though not so fortunate was ships steward, John Almond of Cherry Street, Blackburn, last seen struggling in the chaotic waters after the torpedoing, one of 1,198 fatalities. Across the English Channel however, some of Blackburn's soldiers were in the thick of things engaged in battle at Neuve Chapelle and at Ypres, whilst those in the Blackburn division of the East Lancashire Regiment were reported as doing brilliantly in the Dardenelles area, shortly before this Turkish peninsula was evacuated and the whole campaign regarded a complete failure. For the first time, the war reached British shores when London and East Anglia were subjected to aerial bombardment from Zeppelin raids. In Scarborough several buildings were destroyed by German battleships off the Yorkshire Coast firing on the resort and in Blackburn, fire-hoses were installed throughout the borough in case of incendiary attack. So far as any improvements in the town were concerned, these were put on hold until the ending of hostilities, which included a scheme to construct a new electricity generating station for the town at Whitebirk, although building work continued on the Longshaw mill, which began production during 1915, becoming the last weaving mill to be built in Blackburn. The public halls in Northgate, also under construction when war broke out, remained roofless, though the basement of the buildings were used to accommodate wounded soldiers, transferred from 'Ellerslie', a private house on East Park Road, which having only 25 beds soon exceeded its capabilities. The Union Workhouse was requisitioned by the Military Authorities, converting it into a military hospital, whilst Queen Mary's Military Hospital opened at the unfinished Calderstones Hospital near Whalley to accommodate more of the wounded of this war.

As the Great War moved on into 1916, conscription was introduced to boost the nation's forces still further despite opposition from certain factions of society. At the same time a new phenomenon was being experienced in the cotton trade in Blackburn when 2000 looms lay idle, not for once due to shortages of orders, but for want of hands to ply the looms. Such was the shortage that one cotton operative went unsuccessfully to a military tribunal, seeking an exemption for two male employees from military services due to this shortage of workers. The Blackburn branch of the Women's league was established during this year to provide company

The Union Workhouse, Whinney Heights which became Queen's Park Hospital and which still functions as a hospital. *Photo courtesy of Blackburn Library.*

for those wives and mothers of men away on active service and the death was announced of Mr Robert Armstrong Yerburgh, son-in-law of the late Daniel Thwaites of the Star Brewery, but it was for events on the Battlefields of Europe that the year of 1916 is best remembered, becoming synonymous with one of the most disastrous battles of all time, the infamous Battle of the Somme, a battle intended to punch a hole through German defences which, it was hoped would bring a speedy end to the war.

After the first day of the battle, the press claimed it had been a great day, but as days went on, the dreadful reality began to emerge, 20,000 killed on the first day, 40,000 injured. At first in Blackburn it was difficult to determine the extent of men from the town who had been killed. Eventually, the much feared headline appeared, 'Heavy Death Toll amongst men of Blackburn and District'. Throughout the early part of the war there had been a trickle of names listed in the local newspapers of those soldiers from the town being lost to the war, but in the summer of 1916, this trickle, rapidly gave way to a torrent of names rising steadily by the day, the pages which at the start of the war had pictured battalions eagerly anticipating departing to Europe, had long since been replaced by pictures of individuals who had perished on those battlefields of Europe. A particularly

disturbing feature of the war by this time, was the fact that in minutes whole communities had been robbed of their men tragically highlighting the short-sightedness of the Pals Battalion scheme. Pink Street off Bank Top was one such street where telegram boys had the unenviable task of delivering the dreaded message. Barely a house in this street, escaped the bland and uninformative telegram, conveying the message that loved ones had perished, life-long friends and companions, killed side-by-side, so far away from home, dying in the shadow of the devastated French town of Peronne, unmercifully wrecked by departing German soldiers, who had used it as their regional HQ.

But should the people of Blackburn ever have been in any doubt that the Great War was anything more than a romantic crusade, where the hero goes off to war, and would return a little dishevelled, with a few scratches and a uniform covered in specks of dust, then an event in the town changed all of this, driving home the true realities of war and the indiscriminate slaughter of human life showing that in this war, many of the heroes did not return. Ironically, it was the town's premier music hall, The Palace, which portrayed the truth, by switching from its usual variety programme to 'pictures', screening the renowned film, 'Battle of the Somme', a film using actual footage depicting the battle, interpolated with re-enacted events. Well used to seeing audiences wreathed in mirth, the

The Palace Theatre of Varieties, Boulevard, premier music hall of the MacNaughton Vaudeville Circuit, brought many of the greats of music hall to Blackburn. It was here in 1916 that the theatre switched its programme from variety to moving pictures, screening the renowned film *'Battle of the Somme'* shocking audiences with its graphic depiction of war showing that the Great War was not such a lovely war.
Photo courtesy of Blackburn Library.

walls echoing peels of laughter, this great entertainment house, witnessed vivid depictions of battle, as soldiers left their trenches to go 'over the top' into 'no mans land' only to be mowed down by enemy gunfire. Meant as a public information film and morale booster, the film had quite the opposite effect, horrifying, yet compelling audiences to observe the scale of the carnage, three times a day for a week to packed houses. It was as near the truth that any public information film has been in wartime and was to become, the first and last uncensored war film.

Life in Blackburn was growing increasingly more difficult as the stalemate on the western front continued into 1917 with victory seemingly impossible. Food prices began to increase in response to a reduction of imports, followed by the obligatory impositioning of rationing, administered by the Local Food Control Committee from headquarters in Richmond Terrace. There was a little splash of colour in Blackburn in this year, when the stars and stripes were flown from all of the town's public buildings at the glorious news that the United States had finally entered into this conflict and the hope they could provide the extra push necessary to bring this protracted conflict to an end. The third anniversary of the war passed that August, coinciding with the start of the third Battle of Ypres, the battle taking a second name from a nearby Belgian village in the Flanders region, famous for its poppy fields - Passchendaele. Like the Somme before it, news filtering through to Blackburn of fatalities was sparse, but as the battle continued, the flow of fatalities inundated pages of the town's press with as many of the deaths caused by drowning in the mud as from the effects of shells and bullets.

It was during the Battle of Passchendaele, that Blackburn soldier William Grimbaldeston, became the second man from the town to be awarded the Victoria Cross and the first to receive the French Croix de Guerre decoration in recognition of his bravery. With little armed cover and alone, he gradually advanced to a German pillbox, armed with only a hand gun and grenade. Success was vital if the regiment was to proceed and Grimbaldeston achieved this aim, entering the pillbox and capturing all 36 of its German occupants. Two more Blackburn men were awarded VCs, the following year for their outstanding bravery, Lieutenant Commander Percy Dean for his part in the naval raid of Zeebrugge and Lieutenant John Schofield, who attacked the front line and captured 123 of the enemy being killed in action at Givenchy, King George V awarding his posthumous medal to Lieutenant Schofield's mother, whose other son had been one of the many hundreds from Blackburn killed at the Somme. During that same year the deaths of former Blackburn MP and mill owner, William Coddington and the 'Blackburn Giant', 8'4" Frederick Kempster were announced and news also filtered through that Whalley born, Dr Alexander Macklin, a former house officer at Blackburn Royal Infirmary, had been awarded the Polar Medal for his role in the Ernest Shackleton led, Imperial trans-Antartic Expedition. At the fourth anniversary of the start of the war passed on 4 August 1918 with the conflict entering a fifth year, although the weeks which followed were destined to become the last of the Great War, for after four years and three months, the stalemate on the western front came suddenly to an end.

News of the imminent German surrender was posted in the windows of the newspaper offices in the town, a little after 10:30am on the morning of 11 November 1918, and at 11:00am that same morning, fighting ceased. For many in Blackburn on this great day, the raising of the union flag above buildings throughout the borough was their first notion that the war could be at an end, though many hardly dared think this, since their hopes had been dashed many times by unsubstantiated rumours. As the day progressed many ventured onto the streets of the town of Blackburn to see if it could be true. Yet despite the fact that this most devastating of wars was over, the sufferings were not at an end due to the outbreak of a particularly nasty strain of influenza which swept through the town. This Spanish Flu epidemic had within days of the ending of the war, claimed the lives of nearly 100 people in Blackburn, an epidemic which world-wide killed more people within a month than the whole of the Great War. Before the year was out, there was more reason to celebrate for the women of Blackburn, as 26,000 women in the town were given the vote for the first time, their loyalty and help during the war thus being rewarded. Though it only included married women and those over the age of 30, it was a huge stride forward and a great victory for the suffragette movement who had campaigned tirelessly before the start of the war, to enable women to have the vote.

For the first time since the New Year of 1914, fireworks heralded the arrival of 1919. The first month of the year saw the results of the General Election announced with the Blackburn Labour MP and vociferous pacifist, Philip Snowden losing his seat to Blackburn War hero and VC winner, Lieutenant-Commander Percy Dean and a civic welcome being given for 580 soldiers returning to the town after having being held captive. During April 1919, the 4th Battalion of the East Lancashire Regiment paraded to the Parish Church to reclaim their regimental colours deposited there on the eve of departure for foreign shores in September 1914. More rejoicing followed in July 1919 at news that the Treaty of Versailles, a document attempting to put right the wrongs which had contributed to the start of the war, but which was somewhat prejudiced by the horrors of this war which could not be erased from people's minds, intent on wreaking revenge on those they believed responsible, had been signed, bringing the Great War officially to a close. As a consequence, Germany lost huge amounts of land, was forced to disarm and to reduce the size of its forces. But the Germans like the British and the French, were a patriotic and proud nation and to be humiliated in such a way only paved the way for future conflict. For the time being however, with the prospect of a severely weakened Germany, there seemed little possibility of a war on this scale with Germany ever happening again and at last, the Great War for civilisation, the war to end all wars was finally and officially at an end. People could now look towards a peaceful and hopefully prosperous future and with Blackburn's cotton industry booming things looked very bright for the coming decade.

EVENTS DURING THE GREAT WAR

1914
- Volunteers start to register for war (29 Aug).
- All Germans living in town to register with Police.
- League of Frontiersmen formed in town.
- Local Territorials depart for Foreign Service (12 Sept).
- 'Ellerslie' private house in East Park Road becomes war hospital with 25 beds.
- Blackburn Electricity Committee secure 60 Acres of land at Whitebirk.
- 4th Battalion of East Lanc's Regiment arrive in Egypt (24 Oct).
- Call to Arms meeting at town hall.
- First batch of wounded soldiers arrive in Blackburn, (31 Oct).
- Municipal elections suspended due to war.
- Calls for no fireworks on Bonfire Night.
- Workhouse declared overcrowded.
- Yerburghs return to Blackburn after being stranded in German territory.
- 80lbs of cheese given to poor of Blackburn as gift from Canada.

1915
- Low key celebrations bring in New Year.
- 132 Belgian refugees arrive in Blackburn.
- Blackburn's territorials in battle against Turks near Suez Canal (6 Feb).
- Proposals for new power station at Whitebirk discouraged by Government until war ends.
- Longshaw Mill begins production, the last textile mill to open in Blackburn.
- Motor Ambulances purchased to replace horse-drawn ones.
- Lusitania torpedoed and sunk, Blackburn man amongst the fatalities.
- Fire hoses erected in town in case of incendiary attack.
- Raising of age of military recruits to 40 and drop in height requirement.
- Office set up in Preston New Road, to recruit for Blackburn's Pals Battalion.
- Cadet force formed by Blackburn Recruiting Committee.
- Territorials withdrawn from Galipoli and the Dardenelles.
- Ramsey MacDonald addresses meeting in Blackburn.
- Service held at Parish Church in memory of Edith Cavell.
- Introduction of Automatic stamp machines at GPO.
- GPO unveils role of honour with names of all their employees serving in the forces.

1916
- Introduction of compulsory conscription (1 Jan).
- 9 Blackburn families give 4 or more sons to war.
- 2,000 looms idle for want of hands to work them.

- Visit of Prince Alphonse de Chirmay of Belgium.
- Blackburn branch of Women's league set up to provide company for wives and mothers of those on active service.
- Battle of the Somme (1 Jul), High death toll amongst men from Blackburn.
- Military Authorities requisition Workhouse to use as Military Hospital.
- War shrine dedicated at house in Lucknow Street.
- Death of Robert Armstrong Yerburgh.

1917
- Blackburn Chamber of Commerce urges increase in cotton cultivation within Empire due to shortages.
- Dismissal of case put before military tribunal by cotton operative seeking exemption for two overlookers due to shortages of workers in industry.
- Stars and Stripes flown from every flagstaff in Blackburn as USA enter war.
- Patients transferred from 'Ellerslie' to the unfinished public halls on Northgate.
- Attempt to pull up tramlines on Cherry Tree Route to use elsewhere, stopped.
- Blackburn soldier, William Grimbaldeston awarded the Victoria Cross and the French Croix de Guerre, for exceptional bravery during the Battle of Passchendaele (Jul-Nov).

1918
- YMCA Buffet for soldiers and sailors opened at Blackburn Railway Station.
- William Grimbaldeston arrives home to civic welcome.
- Death of Sir William Coddington of Wycollar Hall, Conservative MP for Blackburn, (1880-1906).
- Captain Alec Maklin of Whalley and Blackburn receives Polar Medal for his part in the Ernest Shackleton led Imperial Trans-Antarctic expedition.
- Death of 'Blackburn Giant', Fred Kempster.
- Second Lieutenant, John Schofield from Blackburn, posthumously awarded the Victoria Cross for capturing 123 of enemy.
- Victoria Cross awarded to Percy Dean of Blackburn for his role in the Naval raid of Zeebrugge.
- Simultaneous raising of Union Flag in Blackburn as Great War ends (11 Nov).
- Spanish Flu epidemic hits town, 90 deaths in a week.
- 26,000 Women in Blackburn vote for the first time in General Election.

1919
- Blackburn Labour MP and pacifist, Philip Snowden loses seat to VC Winner, Percy Dean in General Election.
- 4th Battalion of East Lanc's Regiment ceremoniously parade to parish church to reclaim regiment colours deposited on eve of departure to war.
- £250,000 borrowed to build new electricity generating station at Whitebirk.
- Improvements in cotton industry sees all the town's mills in full production.
- Flags fly throughout the Borough at news that the Treaty of Versailles has been signed, officially ending the Great War.
- As new decade approaches, cotton trade is booming, though many looms are idle due to shortages of hands to work them.

3. THE AFTERMATH OF WAR - 1920-1929

FOLLOWING ON FROM THE RAVAGES of the Great War came the twenties, an age associated with flippancy and having a good time. The decade began with economic boom and ended with the disaster of the Wall Street Crash. It was the decade when soldiers returned not to a land fit for heroes but to a land of unemployment and strikes and an age when war memorials were being unveiled. Society flappers showed their knees, unthinkable twenty years earlier and young men flaunted plus fours and Oxford bags and sped about in motor cars having a spiffing time. It was the decade of the General Strike and the age of jazz and in dance halls, patrons danced the Charleston and the Black Bottom. The continued barrage of movies from the states created new popular heroes, Valentino, Pickford, Chaplin, Fairbanks and Garbo and whilst Jazz was king, Al Jolson was the Jazz Singer in the first synchronised sound-on-vision film. The world of politics witnessed the spectre of extreme nationalism as the National Socialist party was formed in Germany and the Fascists gained their first seats in Italy; prohibition was introduced in the USA and the Irish Free State was established. Science and technology progressed witnessing the discovery of penicillin, the establishment of the first birth-control clinics and first few flickering moments of television in the decade which also saw the setting up of a major twentieth century British institution - the BBC.

It may have seemed that people in Blackburn could now look towards a brighter future with the war over and the dawning of a new era of peace, but for many their battles to cope in the aftermath of this most devastating of wars was far from over. In this period when a land fit for heroes was promised, ex-servicemen joined the unemployment queues and were to be seen begging on street corners in the town, the disabled, the maimed and the shell-shocked an all too familiar sight on the streets of Blackburn. The twenties became a decade which saw the erection of war memorials, though not in homage to the army leaders, but for the first time, the names of ordinary soldiers killed, fighting for their country were recorded for posterity. A roll of honour unveiled in the vestibule of the town hall, listed the names of those killed in the Great War from the Borough. A corner of solace, the Garden of Remembrance was made in Corporation Park and the memorial wing was added to the Royal

Infirmary. At Little Harwood, a memorial clock was unveiled; at Feniscowles, the War Memorial recreation ground was laid and throughout town, churches erected monuments and dedicated windows, fixtures, fittings and furnishings in memory of those in the relevant parishes who had so nobly answered the call for king and country, all in an attempt to ease the sufferings of those who had lost loved ones. Sir Arthur Conan-Doyle lecturing at King George's Hall on the benefits of the Spiritualist movement, advocated communication with the departed as a means of easing some of the distress experienced by the living, providing an opportunity to say goodbye, but for many, a lasting memorial should be the reminder that there should never be a war on the scale of this one again. Two thousand in Blackburn joined a 'No more wars' march through the centre of town, from Northgate to Queens Park gaining numbers all the way and as Blackburn's population began the struggle to come to terms with the devastation of war. The Borough adopted the French town of Peronne in the Somme Department devastated by the Germans, financing a project to rebuild the bridge over the River Somme, 'Le Pont du Blackburn' - The Bridge of Blackburn, providing a link not only across a mighty river, but with a town in whose shadow, so many Blackburnians had lost their lives, so far from home.

Those who did return from war experienced a post-war boom in the cotton industry with all available hands to the looms. Smitten by their sudden wealth, many a mill-owner retired in the relatively secure notion of cotton's prosperity, to places like Blackpool, Lytham

The Garden of Rememberance in *Corporation Park,* created in honour of those from the town who lost their lives in the Great War. *Photo courtesy of Blackburn Library.*

St Anne's and Southport, only to have to return to their mills when disaster struck in 1921 in the form of a dramatic slump, which marked the beginning of the long and savage decline of Blackburn's cotton trade. The war had been a major cause of decline since trade with India was suspended, allowing India's own cotton industry to expand at the expense of our own. Import tariffs imposed by them after the resumption of trade meant that Britain could no longer effectively compete in this field; a devastating blow since Blackburn and Darwen had for many years woven almost exclusively for the Indian Market. By the end of this first year of desperation, a third of the town's looms lay idle as unemployment soared to record levels with many looms never to start up again and then two years later, the Foundry Hill (Soho) and the Limbrick became the first two Blackburn Mills to permanently close.

The high levels of unemployment experienced in Blackburn at this time prompted both the trade's council and the Blackburn branch of the Labour Party, to urge the town council to take action to curb these levels. Consequently, a series of measures were introduced intended to get those unemployed back to work. The redecorating of the town hall and the widening of the borough's roads were two such schemes and further employment was found following the approval of a scheme to construct an arterial road around the outskirts of the town. A far reaching plan to provide work for the unemployed was put before the trades council by the founder of the Northern Daily Telegraph, T.P.Ritzema, who suggested time was ripe to redevelop the town centre, believing there to be a trade recovery just around the corner. Central to the plan was the re-siting of the market to a site between Ainsworth and Penny Street, discussed thirteen years earlier, which got no further than the drawing board. The council was cautious at this time also, since these predictions were not based on any solid evidence. Not sharing Ritzema's optimism for the near future, the council in line with a national policy of caution in respect of investment in costly redevelopment schemes, were not prepared to put such a scheme into action until definite signs of trade recovery were evident. Despite the mood, the new fire station on the Wrangling, the Queen's Hall Methodist Mission, the new St Anne's RC Church, the Salvation Army Citadel, the Infirmary extension, and the Regent (Roxy), Palladium and Savoy Cinemas were all constructed in this cautionary age, which also saw the Exchange Picture Hall, metamorphose into the Majestic Cinema, the public halls and the new electricity generating station at Whitebirk finally completed and the opening of parks at Roe Lee and off Aqueduct

The Public Halls, Northgate, officially opened by Lord Derby in 1921. In the distance is the technical school on Blakey Moor. *Photo courtesy of Blackburn Library.*

Road. On the progress front, there was a little brightness on the horizon with the abolition of the 'half-timer' scheme and wireless usage greatly increased in the town. Sport and recreation also featured at this time with the formation of Blackburn Rugby Club. The increased popularity of lawn tennis prompted the construction of courts at Queen's and Corporation Parks and Blackburn Water Polo team won the English Championships in 1923, with team captain, Richard Hodgson, being selected for the British team, representing the country at the 1924 Paris Olympics.

By the mid-twenties, for those without motor cars, there was the char-a-banc outing to the coastal districts of Lancashire which became a regular treat at the town's annual holiday seasons; ladies dressed in fur collared coats with cloches pulled firmly on heads. This increased use of the internal combustion engine signalled the end of horse-drawn fire engines and ambulances, being replaced by motorised versions and satisfactory trial runs of covered double-deck trams were made. A host of celebrities descended on Blackburn at this time including: Herbert Asquith, David Lloyd George, Sir Robert Baden Powell who attended a scout rally at Witton Park and Home Secretary, Arthur Henderson. Blackburn's temperance queen, Mrs Elizabeth Lewis passed away during 1924 with the town's

Blackburn Boulevard, with char-a-bancs lined up awaiting day trippers. Most popular destinations being Blackpool, the Lake District and Yorkshire Dales. *Photo courtesy of Blackburn Library.*

publicans closing their doors, out of respect for their late adversary on the day of her funeral and two of Blackburn's notable theatre managers, Edward Herman Page and Harry Yorke also made their exit in the early nineteen twenties as did the veteran Liberal Statesman and Freeman of the Borough, Viscount John Morley of Blackburn and former Blackburn Rovers player James Forrest, who set a club record in the FA Cup final of 1891, by winning a fifth FA Cup medal playing for Blackburn Rovers. The town centre lost a mighty landmark during 1925 when the 250 feet chimneystack at the Corporation Electricity Works on Jubilee Street was felled at a time when industry was experiencing a difficult time. The industrial strife

Blackburn Station and the Ribble Bus terminus Blackburn Boulevard.
Photo courtesy of Blackburn Library.

continued into 1926 when a national coal strike escalated into the General Strike crippling industries and communications networks throughout the country. In Blackburn, the publication of newspapers was suspended, with bulletins produced to advise people of the situation and tram, train and other public transport services were halted on the first day, until services were resumed by gangs of volunteers. Although after nine days, the strike ended, the coal dispute continued for a further six months having a devastating effect on the town's already troubled cotton industry, suspending production at half of the town's mills hungry for coal and rendering 12,000 unemployed. Industrial chaos reigned as the Blackburn branch of the Communist Party was formed, the Labour Party leader, Ramsey MacDonald addressed a meeting from the stage of the Palace Theatre and a new concept in shopping was introduced when FW Woolworth and Co. opened their 3d and 6d store in premises on Church Street. It was also during 1926 that the Parish Church celebrated its centenary with news that approval had been given for the church to be upgraded to the status of cathedral, centre of the newly formed Diocese of Blackburn, 1,330 years after Saxon settlers to the area established the very first parish church in Blackburn.

Clear skies gave Blackburn people an uninterrupted view of a very rare and spectacular phenomenon when in June 1927, the first total eclipse of the sun visible from Great Britain for 150 years took place and what in Blackburn may have been observed by some people as an omen of good fortune; the year did see an improvement in the town's cotton trade with a fall in the town's unemployment. At this same time, the enthronement took place of the first Bishop of Blackburn, the Reverend Percy Mark Herbert, the stone drinking fountain in Salford was removed to reduce the problems of traffic congestion there, being relocated at Pleasington Playing Fields and a new industry and valuable employer arrived following the acquisition of the former Witton Roller Skating Rink by the Haslingden based firm, Scapa Dryers, manufacturers of paper makers felts. These improvements in the town's fortunes continued into 1928 as Blackburn Rovers celebrated their 53rd anniversary in fine style, by beating the then invincible Huddersfield Town 3-1 in that year's FA Cup Final, bringing the trophy back to the town for an incredible seventh time, greeted by a crowd of 100,000 on their home-coming, the trophy held aloft by players in an open bus for all to see. Sadly however, the celebrations for the Rovers were marred by a slump in the cotton industry, rendering 35 Blackburn cotton mills idle as the respite in the ill-fortunes of the trade ended and the decline of the

Blackburn Rovers FA Cup Winning Team of 1928, who secured the trophy with their 3-1 win over Huddersfield Town at Wembley. *Photo courtesy of Blackburn Library.*

town's cotton trade resumed once more with a vengeance.

The last year of this decade gave indications of what was to come. A new concept in cinema opened at the Savoy Cinema on Bolton Road, when the all-singing, all-dancing, all talkin', Broadway Melody opened for a two week run, the first talking picture to be shown in Blackburn, 40,000 cotton workers stayed away from work for a week following a request by employers to impose a 12% wage cut and mill closures continued with the closure of eight more mills, bringing the tally in six years to twenty-eight. Barely a year after the extension of the franchise giving women the same voting rights as

'If I had a talking picture...'. *The Savoy Cinema,* Bolton Road, opened in 1922 and in 1929 presented 'Broadway Melody', the first talking picture to be shown in Blackburn. The cinema also boasted car parking, something of a novelty at the time. *Photo courtesy of Blackburn Library.*

men, the Borough's first woman Member of Parliament, Mary Hamilton was one of two Labour MP's elected in the 1929 General Election. A diocesan conference was held also in this year, opening a fund to provide money to enlarge the existing Cathedral, but so far as the much needed redevelopment of the centre of Blackburn was concerned, no further decision was taken, the council continuing to err on the side of caution, especially with the rapid decline of the town's prime industry. This appeared to be a wise move for on 24 October, 1929, came the Wall Street Crash, the shock waves from this event creating a tidal wave of economic disaster in the developed world and the 'Great Depression' was born, not the most promising foundations for the following decade to be built upon.

EVENTS 1920-1929.

1920
- Approval given to build obelisk as war memorial in *St Michael's* church yard.
- Closure of Nova Scotia Brewery following take-over by Matthew Brown and Co. of Preston.
- Regent *(Roxy)* Cinema opened.
- First two municipal houses built on Green Lane.
- Fire at Number 2 Market Hall (Fish Market) causes £50,000 of damage.

1921
- Blackburn Rugby Union FC formed.
- 38 Textile Mills stopped (15 Jan)
- 29,000 unemployed, 90% textile workers, (19 March).
- Inaugural dinner of Blackburn Rotary Club held at *Old Bull Hotel.*
- Adoption of the French towns of Peronne and Maricourt by Blackburn.
- Electricity cables laid in Mill Hill, enabling electricity to be supplied there.
- Closure of the *Thwaites* owned *Snig Brook* Brewery.
- Palladium *'Cinema de lux'*, Mill Hill opened.
- *King George's* Hall and Whitebirk electricity generating station opened by Lord Derby, (22 Oct).
- Death of Edward Herman Page, former manager of the *Lyceum* and *Prince's Theatres.*
- Formation of Blackburn Textile Society.
- Visit of Liberal Leader, Herbert Asquith.
- Purchase of 58 acres of land at Pleasington from Major Feilden for playing fields and recreation grounds.

1922
- Flu epidemic hits the town.
- Unveiling of memorial organ, *King George's* Hall.
- Last half-timer in cotton industry employed.
- Savoy Picture House, Nova Scotia, opened.
- Illumination of Mill Hill Congregational Church clock.
- £20,000 raised in the borough to re-build bridge over the River Somme at Peronne.
- Sir Arthur Conan Doyle addresses meeting at *King George's* Hall on the subject of the future life.
- Municipal tennis courts opened at *Queen's* and *Corporation Parks.*
- Conference in Manchester decides Blackburn to become see town of a new Anglican diocese.
- New Fire Station opened on *Byrom Street.*

1923

- Permanent closure of the Foundry Hill *(Soho)* and the Limbrick Cotton Mills.
- Little Harwood War Memorial Clock unveiled.
- A 'No more wars' march through the centre of Blackburn attracts 2,000 people.
- Blackburn Water Polo Team, wins the English Championship.
- Closure of the Henry Shaw and Co. owned Salford New Brewery.
- Death of Harry Yorke, former manager of the *Theatre Royal*.
- Death of Viscount John Morley of Blackburn, veteran Liberal politician.
- David Lloyd George addresses meeting at the Railway Station.
- Plan to widen the *Borough's* roads begins, to relieve traffic congestion and provide work for the growing number of unemployed.
- Garden of Remembrance, *Corporation Park,* formally opened, (14 Jul).
- Sir Robert Baden Powell, attends scout rally at *Witton Park.*
- Approval given to plan to build arterial road from *Brownhill* to *Whalley Old Road.*
- T.P.Ritzema, founder of the *Northern Daily Telegraph,* suggests plan for improving Blackburn Town Centre, by moving market onto land between Ainsworth and *Penny Street,* to provide work for the unemployed.
- Plan approved for the decorating the town hall and sessions house, providing work for the unemployed.

1924

- *Queen's Hall, Methodist Mission, Darwen Street* opened.
- Closure of the Eanam and *Moss Street* Cotton Mills.
- Decline of invitation to Oswald Mosley by Blackburn Labour Party, to contest the constituency seat at the next general election.
- Visit of evangelist, Gypsy Smith, to the *Queen's Hall.*
- Royal Assent given for the formation of the new Bishopric of Blackburn.
- Unveiling of war memorial statue, *Corporation Park.*
- Horse-drawn fire engines driven out for the last time.
- Death of Mrs Elizabeth Lewis, the *'drunkards friend'* and founder of the Lees Hall, Teetotal Mission, *St Peter Street*.
- *'Le Pont de Blackburn',* Peronne, the bridge financed by the town opened in the presence of the mayor of Blackburn
- Extensively refurbished Exchange Hall, reopens as the *Majestic Cinema.*
- Laying of the foundation stone of the War Memorial Wing of the Infirmary laid by Mrs Elma Yerburgh.
- 150 deaths in Blackburn in one week due to flu epidemic.
- Richard Hodgson, captain of Blackburn's Water Polo team selected for the British Olympic team.

1925

- Death of James Kenyon, cinema pioneer.
- Closure of the Nova Scotia, Bridge and Mill Hill Cotton Mills.
- Golden Jubilee of Blackburn Rovers.
- *St Mary's* RC College founded by the Marist Fathers.
- Replacement of horse-drawn ambulances by motorised ones.
- White lines painted on roads throughout the Borough in an attempt to minimise traffic accidents.
- Foundation of *St Marks* Conservative Club, Witton, laid by Major Feilden.
- Memorial cross unveiled on the grave of Mrs Elizabeth Lewis, by John Oats, the first man to *'sign the pledge'* with her.
- Demolition of electricity generation station chimney, *Jubilee Street.*
- *Salvation Army Citadel, Vicar Street, Salford,* opened.
- Colours of the 4th Battalion of the East Lancashire Regiment represented after being inscribed with battle honours from the Great War.
- Satisfactory trials of the first covered double-deck trams.

- Closure of *Victoria Brewery, Mary Ann Street.*

1926
- Blackburn branch of the *Communist Party* established.
- Opening of the *FW Woolworth and Company* owned *'3d and 6d Store',* in *Church Street.*
- Percy Mark Herbert, appointed first Bishop of Blackburn.
- Town's industry crippled by national coal strike.
- Publication of census figures, show a fall in the town's population of almost 15,000 in ten years.
- Industry, communications and transport brought to a standstill as the coal dispute erupts into the General Strike, (4-12 May).
- Closure of *Greaves Street* Cotton Mill.
- Centenary of Parish Church with news it is to be upgraded into Blackburn Cathedral.
- Ramsey MacDonald addresses meeting at the *Palace Theatre.*

1927
- The new diocese of Blackburn officially comes into being.
- New *St Anne's* RC Church, *Paradise Lane* opens.
- Acquisition of the former *Witton Roller Skating Rink, Cartmel Road,* by Scapa Dryers of Haslingden.
- Unemployment falls to lowest level in two years.
- Stone drinking fountain, Salford, removed to *Pleasington Fields.*
- First total eclipse of the sun, visible in Great Britain for 203 years visible from the town.
- Enthronement of the first Bishop of Blackburn.
- Matthew Brown and Co. of Preston, take over the *Lion Brewery of Nuttall's, Little Harwood.*
- Closure of the *Fountain Free Brewery,* Red Cap.

1928
- *Prince's Theatre, Jubilee Street,* renamed, *'The Grand'.*
- Blackburn Rovers win the FA Cup for the sixth time, beating Huddersfield 3-1 at Wembley Stadium, 100,000 turn out to welcome the team home.
- Sale of the *Swan Brewery,* Larkhill, to Dutton's.
- Slump in Cotton industry, renders 35 mills in the town idle.
- War Memorial Wing, Royal Infirmary, opened by Mrs Elma Yerburgh.

1929
- 40,000 operatives stay away from work, following employers request to impose 12% wage reduction.
- General Bramwell Booth addresses meeting at the *Palace Theatre.*
- Fund launched to finance scheme to extend the Cathedral.
- Roll of Honour unveiled in the vestibule of the town hall, with names of those from the town who died in the Great War.
- *'Broadway Melody',* the first talking picture shown in the town, opens for a two week run at the Savoy Cinema.
- Mary Hamilton (Labour), becomes the town's first woman Member of Parliament.
- BBC visits Blackburn Technical College to demonstrate broadcasting.
- First Labour Mayor of Blackburn, Luke Bates is selected.
- Radium fund launched at Blackburn Infirmary.
- Summer heatwave, temperatures reach 80 degrees in July.
- Record gates at Alexandra Meadows, see Nelson Cricket Club pro, Leary Constantine.
- *Wall Street Crash,* plunges world into economic depression, (24 Oct).
- Closure of ten mills in two months as unemployment rises to 9,200.
- This decade of hope ends in a state of gloom as people are forced to use up savings to survive.

4. DEPRESSION AND THE ROAD TO WAR - 1930 - SEPTEMBER 1939.

BUILT ON THE LEGACY OF THE CRASH OF '29, the thirties became an age associated with depression and dole queues, strikes and mass unemployment and of poverty and despair. The nation mourned the passing of one monarch, observed the abdication of a second and celebrated the coronation of a third, whilst watching with consternation, the antics of Adolf Hitler as he blatantly contravened the terms and conditions of the Treaty of Versailles. They flocked in their millions to the new-styled picture palaces to see their idols of the silver screen and cheered Chamberlain's promise that there would be no second European War.

It was the state of Blackburn's cotton industry, which dominated the news in 1930. The decade followed on where the twenties left off, the Crash of '29 being to Blackburn, little more than another factor in the decline of the town's industrial base. Things looked anything but healthy for the textile trade, since at the start of the year of 1930, unemployment numbered 21,000 with 50 mills stopped entirely, and this had risen to 100 mills idle by June of that year. Unemployment remained the scourge of the early thirties, as each week, dole queues grew ever-longer, as did peoples hardship and despair, since there seemed no easy nor ready solution to this problem. The spectacular decline of Blackburn's cotton industry continued throughout, with a total of 26 mills permanently closing between 1930 and 1934. As unemployment lurched towards the 30,000 mark, out of a working population of almost 80,000, an unsuccessful attempt was made to gain Government funding to attract new industries to the town. In a bid to prevent further mill closures, wage reductions and short-time working were imposed resulting in strike action, but with the prospect of poverty knocking at the door, compromises as such were being reluctantly accepted as the lesser of the two evils.

The fear that Blackburn was beginning to die was further exacerbated by the 1931 census, showing there to be a fall in the town's population by over 4,000 in ten years, the second consecutive fall, increasing as the grip of the depression became even tighter, prompting people to leave the town in search of better prospects. The United States was one option, seen as the land of opportunity and though many set out on this venture to make their fortunes, not all achieved their dream. Nearer to home, others left for Coventry and Luton for the car industry, prospering at that time. In Blackburn, various schemes were introduced for those who couldn't afford to take up such opportunities to get the long-term unemployed back working. Hundreds were employed on schemes in such areas of urban regeneration. A new sewage pipeline was constructed to sewage works at Samlesbury, together with the continuation of improvements to the borough's roads, so that the arterial road ran from Accrington Road to Bolton Road, Ewood, carrying traffic around the outsides edges of the town without having to pass through the town centre. In these hungry years £100 was donated by Mrs. Elma Yerburgh, to provide soup for the unemployed and the good-will of the townsfolk extended where people could afford, taking the opportunity to have their homes improved - decorated by unemployed decorators and some having bathrooms and inside WCs installed, providing work for unemployed plumbers. Community House, a centre for the unemployed was established at the disused St Matthews School, where unemployed cotton workers were taught new skills, such as wood working and undertaking work to benefit the community as a whole. Choral singing and plays were also encouraged, with members providing scenery and from this, the town's Community Theatre came into being.

By the end of 1932, the number of unemployed in Blackburn had peaked and by the beginning of 1933, a reduction in these figures had been recorded. Despite the fall the suffering and despair continued as housewives still had the difficult task of making ends

The Arterial Road at Brownhill, part of the Ring Road scheme constructed during the 1930's to alleviate traffic congestion in the town centre. Garden fronted houses line the road which passes St. Gabriels Church at the top of the brow, all products of the 1930's. *Photo courtesy of Blackburn Library Municipal.*

meet, fearing a visit from the dreaded means-test man. The misery associated with this period was further intensified when Blackburn Rovers were relegated, to the second division for the first time in the club's history. In this atmosphere of gloom and despondency, the Corporation bus station at Intack opened followed by the withdrawal of electric trams firstly on the Audley/Queen's Park route, followed by withdrawal on the Cherry Tree Route, being replaced by buses, built in the town at East Lancashire Coachbuilders. The thirties also bade farewell to the sounding of the town's one o'clock gun, the Peel Buildings on King William Street and the venerable Theatre Royal and mourned the deaths of the founder of the Northern Daily Telegraph, Thomas Ritzema, and two of the town's former MPs, Percy Dean, VC and Philip Snowden. Mill Hill Mill was demolished, the site of the mill's lodge being transformed into Mill Hill Gardens, Griffin Lodge, formerly the home of the mill-owning Dugdale family was acquired by the Corporation, its gardens opened up to the public and land at Livesey behind St Andrews School was turned into a memorial playing fields in honour of the late King George V. The town's premier hotel, the Old Bull closed, the architecturally modernistic St Gabriel's Church at Brownhill was consecrated and fearing that Blackburn's cotton industry might disappear completely, local industrialist T.Lewis opened a textile museum on Exchange Street. On the outlying rural districts of town, a housing programme was under way during the thirties, building high quality, semi-detached houses each with their own individual gardens, creating a

The Rialto Luxury Cinema, Penny Street, in the 1930s, '40s and 50s, the largest cinema in Blackburn. *Photo courtesy of Blackburn Library.*

suburbia, at outlying districts such as Livesey, Cherry Tree, Lammack and Pleckgate.

Though for many, times were hard throughout the thirties and money was scarce, the dream palaces were for many, their only escape from the realities of the depression. In the wake of developments in the talking picture, a new class of cinema emerged - the 'super cinema', the emphasis being on luxury and comfort dealing the final blown to the town's theatres and music halls, whose audience numbers had been dwindling for many years. Both the Theatre Royal and the Grand (ex-Princes) made the switch to talkies, though the Palace faced an uncertain future following the theatre's closure during the summer of 1932, just as live entertainment was re-introduced next door at the Grand. The Association of British Properties built the town's first super cinema - the mighty Rialto (Odeon) in 1931, a splendid building with its capacity of 1,878, making it Blackburn's largest, boasting plush carpets, comfortable seating, show-piece 'Compton' organ, ever-changing Holophane lighting and 150 seat restaurant. An extensively refurbished Palace re-opened in 1936 as the town's second super cinema, whilst plans for a third on Ainsworth Street were abandoned following the announcement that the Theatre Royal was to be demolished and re-built, opening as the Cinema Royal in May 1938, with its high-class restaurant rivalling the established County Café as the place to be seen, taking afternoon tea.

The town was brightened during the thirties by a host of visitors from Royalty and big named celebrities to the famous and the

Church Street, c1930 looking towards Salford and Eanam. *Photo courtesy of Blackburn Library.*

infamous. In 1935, King George V and Queen Mary visited Blackburn as part of their Silver Jubilee tour of the country. Princess Helena Victoria, cousin of the king and granddaughter of Queen Victoria visited Blackburn, to lend her support to the efforts of the town's YWCA, setting up a fund to provide finances to feed starving women in the town and to provide them with useful skills to enable them to regain employment away from cotton. The Dukes of Kent and Gloucester also visited Blackburn as did the Princess Royal, Princess Mary, who came to lay the foundation stone of the cathedral extensions and eighteen months after being catapulted onto the throne by the abdication of Edward VIII, Blackburn was honoured by a visit from King George VI and Queen Elizabeth.

Other visitors to Blackburn during the 30s included Gracie Fields, Anna Neagle, Charlie Chaplin, Alan Cobham and his flying circus, Paul Robeson and Lady Baden Powell. Political visitors included the

Blackshirts and Union of British Fascists leader, Oswald Mosley and his minister of propaganda, William Joyce, (Lord Haw-Haw), who began their recruiting drive at Blackburn and also Prime Minister, Neville Chamberlain who addressed a well attended meeting at King George's Hall in February 1939.

As events in Europe, following the election of Adolf Hitler preoccupied the minds of those in Government, measures were being taken in preparation for war. It was only a few months after Hitler's election to power, that the Blackburn branch of the Air-raid

The Old Bull Hotel, built on the junction of Darwen Street and Church Street, closed as a hotel in 1931, becoming the Headquarters of the ARP wardens in 1938. *Photo courtesy of Blackburn Library.*

Precautionary Committee was established with headquarters at the Old Bull Hotel, followed by a women's division the following year. The possibility of a second European war, proved to be an 'ill wind' for Blackburn. The arrival in the town of a handful of German Jews, fleeing the nazi regime was particularly welcome since they brought with them entrepreneurial expertise and set up factories in the town, providing much needed work for the unemployed of the town As the dark clouds of war gathered on the horizon, action was being taken to increase Britains armaments. Since it was feared this war would be a very different type of war with aerial bombardments, the country's major cities were considered to be high risk targets, whereas the fact that Blackburn was of little strategic value worked in the town's favour. A gas mask factory opened at the former Garden Street Mill during 1937, with the capability for manufacturing half-a-million gas masks a week. That same year the Ministry of War built a Fuse factory near Black-a-moor and Philips electrical components of Mitcham built a production plant at Little Harwood. Yet even so, on his visit to Blackburn, Neville Chamberlain was still hammering home the rallying call 'Peace in our time', the message he brought back following the Munich Crisis, just four months before his visit. But time was fast running out, for just three weeks later after Chamberlain visited, Hitler went against his agreement at Munich and annexed Czechoslovakia; the National Government's appeasement policy was abandoned and Britain geared up for the inevitable war. As the possibility of war increased so too did the demand for labour in Blackburn taking the town full speed out of the Depression.

Upturn in Blackburn's fortunes meant that the town council could at last look at redeveloping the centre of town. However apart from the building of two new cinemas, administration offices for the Electricity Board on Jubilee Street, a new office for the Inland Revenue on Regent Street, new stores for Woolworths, Marks and Spencer and the Co-operative Society on Northgate, following a tradition of slotting new buildings into rows of much older properties and the laying of the foundations of the cathedral extensions, Blackburn's town centre remained little altered, when Hitler's warriors marched into Poland and all plans for the future were put on indefinite hold as war came a little faster than anticipated.

EVENTS 1930-AUGUST 1939.

1930
- 21,000 unemployed, highest since 1920 and still rising, (Jan). 50 mills idle.
- Plans approved to establish libraries at *Mill Hill* and *Whalley New Road.*
- Unemployment surges to 30,000, 100 mills idle, (14 Jun).
- *Grand Theatre* becomes a cinema.
- Scheme to extend market hall proposed.
- Blackburn Golf Club wins Association Trophy for the first time.
- New *Co-operative Emporium,* Northgate, opens.
- Foundations for the new *St Mary's College* laid, on the site of the former Blackburn Olympic Football Ground, at the top of *Shear Brow.*
- Conference to decide how best to compete with foreign competition in the cotton trade.
- Approval of plan to build new sewer to Samlesbury.
- Blackburn's Kathleen Ferrier wins gold medal in the piano competition of the *Liverpool Music Festival.*
- Permanent closure of seven of the town's mills.

1931
- Preliminary census results reports fall in the town's population from 126,922 to 122,695 in ten years.
- Introduction of Means testing.
- Mayor of Blackburn and Secretary of the Weavers' Association go to London to meet the PM, Ramsey MacDonald, to discuss the situation in the cotton industry.
- 2,000 unemployed, demonstrate outside the town hall.
- After almost 150 years, live entertainment comes to an end at the Theatre Royal, as cinema is introduced there.
- Blackburn's largest cinema, the 1878 seat, Rialto Luxury Cinema, (Odeon), opens on Penny Street.

1932
- Drive by council to attract new industry to Blackburn begins.
- 20,000 weavers in Blackburn strike at the imposition of wage cuts.
- Closure of the *Palace Theatre.*
- Scheme approved to supply electricity to Tockholes.
- Employees at *Didsbury Street Mill,* reluctantly accept, 6.5% wage cut.
- Live entertainment returns to the *Grand Theatre.*
- Plan approved to remove the one o'clock gun.
- *Majestic Cinema* sold to *Association of British Cinemas, (ABC).*
- Permanent closure of four more mills.

1933
- New church of *St Gabriel, Brownhill* consecrated.
- Florence Mill reopens after stoppage, with scheme where operatives work for one week at a time, followed by one week off, to double their workforce.
- Introduction of new telephone system in Blackburn, first of its kind with 53 boxes.
- Visit of *Sir Alan Cobham's Flying Circus.*

1934
- Buses replace trams on the *Audley/Queen's Park* route.

- Demolition of *Peel Buildings, King William Street,* to make way for new *Mark's and Spencer's Store.*
- Failure of town's bid to gain upgrade into city.
- Blackburn branch of the YWCA opened to provide food for the starving women of the town.
- Visit of *Princess Helena Victoria,* in support of the YWCA.
- Closure of the *Ordnance and Alexandra* Cotton Mills.
- Visit of Paul Robeson to *King George's* Hall.
- Virulent case of smallpox breaks out, 14 cases.

1935
- Approval of plan to build aerodrome at Samlesbury.
- King George V and Queen Mary visit the town as part of their Silver Jubilee tour of the country.
- Freedom of the Borough conferred on Mrs Elma Yerburgh.

1936
- *New Empress Ballroom,* Town Hall Street opens.
- Sale of Corporation tramway's office, Church Street, to *Woolworth's,* to extend existing store
- Visit of Prince George, Duke of Kent.
- Approval of plan to build *Ritz* super cinema, *Ainsworth Street.*
- Death of George V, oath of allegiance to King Edward VIII sworn.
- Oswald Mosley, Blackshirts leader addresses meeting at King George's Hall.
- Former Palace Theatre reopened as Blackburn's second super cinema.
- Mill Hill Gardens formally opened on site of former mill lodge.
- Arrival in Blackburn of a handful of German Jews fleeing Nazi regime.
- Relegation of Blackburn Rovers to the second division for the first time.
- Abdication of Edward VIII, the Duke of York, proclaimed, King George VI

1937
- Gas Mask factory opens at the former *Garden Street* Cotton Mill off Bank Top.
- *Old Bull* bought by grocers, *EH Booth* to convert into shop.
- Visit of Lady Baden Powell.
- Announcement of plan by the Department of War, to build fuse factory in Blackburn employing 2-2,500 people.
- Death of Philip Snowden, Blackburn's first Labour MP, (1906-1918), aged 72.
- Celebrations mark the coronation of King George VI and Queen Elizabeth.
- Demolition of *Theatre Royal, Ainsworth Street* to make way for new cinema.
- Purchase of *Griffin Lodge,* by *Corporation* to turn grounds into park.
- Visit of Prince Henry, Duke of Gloucester.
- *Philips Electrical* of Mitcham, purchase land at *Little Harwood,* to build production plant there, employing, 4-5000 people.
- Reports of wage increases in cotton industry.
- Blackburn's *Air raid Precautions Committee* established.
- Year ends on a high with 4000 less people unemployed than year before.

1938
- Women's section of air raid wardens founded.
- Introduction of one-way traffic system to alleviate traffic congestion in the town.
- Visit of Princess Mary, the Princess Royal, to lay the foundation stone of the Cathedral extensions, the event broadcast live on *BBC Northern Radio Station.*
- Land at Livesey sold by Elma Yerburgh as Memorial Recreation playing fields in honour of

George V.
- Plan approved to convert the grounds of *Pleasington Hall* into a cemetery.
- *Cinema Royal* and Café opens, *Ainsworth Street.*
- Death of TP Ritzema, founder of the *Northern Daily Telegraph.*
- Construction of new *Woolworth's* store under way.
- *Old Bull* Hotel sold by *EH Booths* to council.
- *Spring Lane* section of arterial road, formally opened.
- Visit of King George VI and Queen Elizabeth.
- *Lewis's Textile Museum* opened, *Exchange Street.*
- Visit of Gracie Fields.
- Central redevelopment scheme discussed.
- Munich Crisis - precautionary measures taken in Blackburn, against air attack, including the digging of trenches to accommodate 15,000 and distribution of 114,000 gas masks from the ARP wardens HQ at the Old Bull Hotel (29 Sept).

1939
- Withdrawal of trams on *Cherry Tree Route.*
- Anna Neagle visits *Rialto Cinema.*
- Blackburn Rovers win promotion to Division 1.
- PM, Neville Chamberlain addresses meeting at *King George's Hall.*
- Blackout tests tried.
- First batch of 20 year olds are called up under Military Service Act, (15 Jul).
- Acid bomb explodes in a pillar-box in *Victoria Street,* believed to be the work of the IRA.
- Two C of E schools, *St Peters* and *St Hildas* opened.
- Death of Percy Dean, former MP and VC holder.
- New electricity administration offices, *Jubilee Street* open.
- German invasion of Poland, (1 Sept).

Wharncliffe Books
FREEPOST SF5
47 Church Street
BARNSLEY
South Yorkshire
S70 2BR

Wharncliffe

If you would like to receive information about other Wharncliffe Books please supply your name, address and special interest areas and return this POST FREE card to us.

Mr/Mrs/Ms ....

Address ....

.... Postcode ....

E-mail address ....

Trade enquiries please tick []   Telephone: 01226 734555

I am particularly interested in - please tick special interest areas:

Aspects Series [] Transport History []
Industrial History [] Entertainment (Theatre & Cinema) []
Local Interest [] Places to Visit []

Wharncliffe

5. BLACKBURN AT WAR - SEPTEMBER 1939 - 1945.

BARELY TWENTY YEARS HAD PASSED after the end of the war to end all wars, before Britain and France were once again at war with Germany, despite the measures taken to prevent such large-scale massacre ever happening again. Unlike the First World War, civilians found themselves in the front line in this period of shortages and rationing, cold winters and fuel crises, but despite the despair of this war, it became a period remembered for the great resilience of the British and their good will towards one another. Everyone pulled together for the good of their country, all subjected, despite rank, to the same hardships and all, standing like a rock in the face of an aggressor who showed no mercy but but whose defeat six years later heralded the start of a period of reconstruction, where peoples pre-war experiences of a bitter society, turned towards a vision of a better society. In the aftermath of the war, the Labour Party swept the prewar National Government into oblivion with a massive electoral majority as troops were united in their aim not to restore the old order, but to instigate a change for the better and to create a land fit for heroes, unfulfilled after the First World War.

On the morning of Friday 1st September 1939, came news both of the German invasion of Poland and of the Prime Minister Neville Chamberlain's ultimatum, demanding their withdrawal by 11:00am on the 3rd. Shortly after 11:00am on that Friday morning, the first trainload of evacuees arrived from Manchester. It was an emotional scene on Blackburn Station that day as children equipped with gas masks and haversacks, displayed a range of emotions from bewilderment to a sense of excitement and adventure, many leaving their homes and parents for the first time. As the evacuees arrived in the relative safety of Blackburn, the first detachment of reservist soldiers were leaving, as their fathers had done, a generation ago, moving off to the unknown. Many who observed the scene at the railway station that morning being moved to tears, especially old soldiers who knew what it was to be setting off on an unknown destiny, as they had done, twenty-five years earlier, when they went off in the belief that they were fighting the war to end all wars, their sadness tinged with the dreadful reality that they had failed.

On the morning of September 3rd 1939, the nation gathered around their radios with dread in their hearts. At Blackburn

Cathedral, the service was interrupted when the provost, the Reverend William Kay, carried a wireless set to the front of the middle aisle. At 11:00 am, the deadline expired, the town of Blackburn like the rest of the country fell silent to listen to Neville Chamberlain's fateful message to the nation, that Britain was once again at war with Germany. For a second time all plans for the future were put on hold as Britain moved into this second war with Germany.

For the first few days, everyone was wrapped up in anticipation, expecting the worst, but apart from the sounding of air raid sirens immediately following Chamberlain's address to the nation, nothing happened. All cinemas, dance halls, theatres and schools were closed, whilst the Government assessed the situation. On 9 September, all re-opened, cinemas in particular were regarded as a valuable commodity, reinforcing morale and providing a welcome for servicemen stationed in Blackburn. The war years became the glory years of Blackburn's cinemas, which by the start of the war had swelled to fourteen. A barrage of quality films provided Blackburn's cinema-going audiences with such timeless classics as: 'Wizard of Oz', 'Goodbye Mr Chips', 'How Green is my Valley', 'Rebecca', 'Pride and Prejudice', 'Jane Eyre', 'Easter Parade', 'The Four Feathers', 'Citizen Kane' and many, many more. In 1943 alone, 'Mrs Minniver', 'Random Harvest', 'Casablanca' and one of the most successful films of all time, 'Gone With the Wind', all made their Blackburn debut at the Majestic Cinema in King William Street, which by that time was under the auspices of the ABC Cinemas group.

Live theatre also enjoyed a revival in fortunes, with the town's Grand Theatre doing good business. King George's Hall provided the venue for the Sunday night variety show, 'Garrisons Theatre' which ran during the winter months from 1940-1945, providing entertainment on Sundays the only day when the town's cinemas were prohibited to open, all revenue from the show going towards the war effort. Dancing was also popular at King George's Hall and there was also dancing at 'Tony's New Empress Ballroom' and the 'Emporium Ballroom, both in Town Hall Street, 'The Palais de Danse' at Sudell Cross, the 'R.O.F. Club', above Burton's shop in New Market Street, 'Alec Marsden's' in Randall Street, plus many other school, church and assembly hall throughout the borough, with music being provided by three and four piece bands. The annual Easter Fair was also seen as vital to morale, though like everything else was subjected to the same constraints including restrictions on noise level and shortages of pottery for the Pot Fair. To combat the Blackout, tarpaulin sheets were drawn around the outsides of rides to prevent lights being shown and to enable the fair to continue as normally as was possible.

In these days of the 'phoney war', when little apart from the mobilisation of troops happened, it wasn't difficult to remember that there was a war on with rationing, the black-out in force and many sons, husbands and brothers were away on active service. Once again, women were drafted into vital war work in Blackburn, keeping the home fires burning once more. For the first time in twenty years, unemployment was virtually zero, the problem like the First World War, being the shortage of people to employ, a feature unthinkable in the darkest days of the Great Depression, less than ten years before. Many women had been drafted into the fuse factories both at Blackburn and Euxton near Chorley, the daily Euxton bus being a feature of those days, ferrying workers to the factory. Other women were drafted into 'Philips' at Little Harwood, the English Electric Works at Clayton-le-Moors and into Blackburn's foundries and engineering factories. Blackburn's disused textile mills were put to good use for a number of purposes. Wellington Mill on Bolton Road became barracks for the West Kent Regiment, complete with sentry on duty at the mill gates and Brookhouse Mill was used for similar purposes. Weaving was placed on the list of essential production for the war, although weaving was suspended at the Malvern, Haston Lee, Royal and India Mills, following their requisition by the

The Northgate side of King George's Hall photographed during the 1940's. Note the sandbag protection for the ground floor, though there is apparently no blast tape on the upper floor windows. It is also interesting to note the white bumpers and running boards on vehicles as an aid to visibility in the blackout. *Photo courtesy of Blackburn Library.*

Ministry of Supply who used these and some of the town's other disused mills as stores.

The winter of 1940 was the first of three bitterly cold winters, the coldest for many years, testing the resilience of the nation in the face of rationing and fuel restrictions. For three days, snow fell heavily and consistently, creating drifting up to roof level in some parts of Blackburn. With no snow clearing facilities available, snow lay on the ground for weeks and the Tockholes bus was abandoned and stood stranded on Morris Brow. By the late spring, the thaw had set in and with it came the transition period as the phoney war moved into action with the fall of Denmark, Norway, Holland, Belgium and finally France, followed by the evacuation of Allied forces at Dunkirk. With much of northern Europe under Nazi control and the threat of invasion more an inevitability than a possibility, the Blackburn branch of the Home Guard was mobilised in response to the country's new Prime Minister, Winston Churchill's call. A Spitfire fund was launched in the town, raising £14,000 in just eight weeks, sufficient to finance the construction of two Spitfires, named Blackburn 1 and Blackburn 2. In response to the Scrap for Victory campaign, ornamental railings were removed from the town's parks as were the Russian canons at Corporation Park, captured at Sebastopol during the Crimean War, the bandstands at both

The Blackburn Division of the Home Guard, formed in response to a call by Winston Churchill to defend the town in the event of an invasion. The Home Guard popularly known as 'Dad's Army', are pictured here parading down Darwen Street, during the Wings for Victory Week. *Photo courtesy of Blackburn Library.*

Corporation and Queen's Parks, together with tons of metal of all shapes and sizes donated by the people of Blackburn in the belief that they were contributing to the war effort.

The late summer of 1940 saw the Battle of Britain, followed by the bombing of Britain's cities: London, Coventry, Bristol, Liverpool, Manchester and Plymouth amongst those badly damaged. In terms of war damage, Blackburn escaped the ravages of the Blitz with only slight damage, although the Nazi propagandist and Radio Hamburg broadcaster, Lord Haw Haw periodically reminded Blackburnians over the airwaves that they hadn't been forgotten by the Nazi's who were quite aware of the Ordnance factory in the town. Two were killed and eight injured when a bomb fell on Ainsworth Street during September 1940. Another bomb fell on Bennington Street destroying a house, the occupiers escaping unhurt and a line of bombs fell in fields to the south of Livesey Branch Road, in direct line of the fuse factory, but missing the target by two miles. But although Blackburn didn't experience the true extent of the bombing, the dreadful realities of the blitz could be observed from the town. The black-out provided the perfect backdrop against which a strangely sinister, sickening orange glow in the night sky to the south of the town, illuminated the nights on which Manchester and Liverpool burned following their extensive bombing. And this coupled with the eerie drone of the Luftwaffe flying over Blackburn, once they had wreaked their deadly havoc, together with the sound of the ack-ack guns at Stanhill, firing indiscriminately into the black in retaliation for the devastation of those cities.

Inspecting the damage. The war comes to Blackburn when a bomb falls on Ainsworth Street in September 1940 killing two people. *Photo courtesy of Blackburn Library.*

As the war continued into 1941, rationing was extended to include clothes. As proof that Blackburn had not been forgotten, King George VI and Queen Elizabeth visited in recognition of the town's efforts for the war, calling in at the R.O.F., and the Home Secretary Herbert Morrison also stopped by. During this year, the BBC broadcast "Workers Playtime" from the Philips plant at Little Harwood and Ewood Park provided the venue for that year's war-time FA Cup final between Arsenal and Preston North End - the Rovers being runners up in the previous year. Though attempts were made to keep the nation's morale as high as possible, these truly were the darkest days in the history of Great Britain. The Nazi invasion of Russia, eased the situation somewhat, bringing a respite to the blitz and the bombing of Pearl Harbor in December 1941, brought the United States into the war on the side of the Allies, but opened up another front and introduced a new aggressor in the form of the Japanese, whose fighting methods were based upon fanaticism, seizing some of the jewels of the British Empire. As each day passed more bad news was announced, the loss of Hong Kong, Malaysia, Singapore, the sinking of the Prince of Wales and Repulse and the constant stream of news of yet more of the town's men being killed in action or being captured by a merciless enemy.

Into 1942, and the early part of the year continued in a similar way to the last with news of further defeats and losses and very little to cheer about. The year began with yet another cold winter, forcing the open market to be abandoned for the first few weeks of January and there was more bad news for the town when Blackburn's adopted cruiser, HMS Naiad was sunk in the Mediterranean. 'Holidays at Home' was introduced in this year, a week of organised events with a fun fair in Corporation Park, in an attempt to cheer up the town's population during the town's wakes week. Finally some good news filtered through in the latter part of 1942, when after two years of silence, church bells were rung throughout the borough in celebration of the Allied victory in Egypt.

By the start of 1943, the threat of a Nazi invasion of Britain was subsiding and restrictions were eased a little allowing the bells of Blackburn's churches to be rung at anytime and blackout restrictions were relaxed slightly, allowing the operation of 'starlight' street lighting at busy areas of town, which could be extinguished at the flick of a switch, should an air raid be imminent. By September, there was more rejoicing in celebration of Italy's unconditional surrender, with flags flying high throughout the borough.

The death of Major James Feilden of Witton Park, Lord of the

Manor of Blackburn was announced in what was to become the historic year of 1944, the year Blackburn was invaded, though not by foe, but by the 'Yanks' who had been barracked at the disused Hornby's Brookhouse Mill, in preparation of the eagerly awaited, invasion of Europe. Their stay albeit brief, added a little vitality, excitement, colour and hope, leaving an indelible mark on a town worn down by the effects of depression and war, but still capable of summoning enough energy to survive and greet the light at the end of this long and very dark tunnel which was beginning to emerge. The presence of the GI, caused consternation for many a mother, whose daughters were captivated by these smooth talking, dynamic yanks, whose cash overflowed the pockets of well cut uniforms and their frighteningly high levels pheromone. It was a brief interlude and as the invasion of Europe came closer, the yanks and other soldiers left the town as quickly as they had arrived. In anticipation of the invasion of Europe, the Royal Infirmary was put on red alert to deal with casualties, then on 6 June 1944, the long awaited news came, D-Day had come, Allied forces had landed on the beaches of Normandy and the liberation of Europe had begun. After almost five years, it eventually looked like the war would be coming to an end with the liberation of the lowlands of Europe. In retaliation, Nazis utilised flying bombs, and in the early hours of Christmas Day 1944, the whole of Blackburn was awoken by a massive explosion shaking the town and surrounding area to its very foundations as a doodlebug fell in the Gregson Lane area of Hoghton over five miles away, killing an elderly lady in a dastardly act, totally against international convention - a desperate act by a fast decaying regime in the face of

Victory Parade, 1945 marching down Preston New Road, pictured here passing the saluting dais outside the gates of Corportation Park.
Photo courtesy of Blackburn Library.

defeat only a matter of weeks away. But so far as the Second World War and Blackburn was concerned, this was to be the last contact the town had with the Nazis as their influence in the world was rapidly disintegrating.

There was a sense of real hope as the New Year of 1945 dawned, yet Blackburn was struck with familiar hardship once again in the form of another bitterly cold winter. The problem was so bad that further fuel rationing was imposed and there was at one stage the real danger that some people would have to do without. The shortages of coke and coal placed the town's bakeries in a desperate situation unable to provide sufficient quantities of bread. With Allied forces moving swiftly through Northern Europe, the town Council began to look once more towards the future, discussing a variety of schemes to be implemented once the war had ended, including improvements to the existing sewerage system, the construction of a crematorium at the recently opened Pleasington Cemetery, new road schemes, the revival of the plan to withdraw the borough's trams and the purchase of Witton Park from the Feilden family. A civic development committee also recommended the demolition of empty property in the Water Street and Old Chapel Street areas between Ainsworth Street and Penny Street in view of commencing the redevelopment of the town centre. Other news during the early part of 1945 included the deaths of three notable people of the town, the noted violinist E Romaine O'Malley, mill magnate, William Birtwistle and the itinerant street entertainer Richard Thompson, alias 'Strong Dick'. But it was events away from the town which continued to dominate the news as the Allies proceeded into the heart of Germany, drawing ever-closer to Berlin and the seat of the fast decaying Nazi power base. Then the great and glorious news came; Germany had surrendered. After six years, Victory in Europe declared and the European stage of the war was at an end. Flags and bunting decorated the town as street parties taking place and people danced in the street celebrating the glorious news.

With the war in Europe over, there began a mass election campaign for the first General Election in ten years. Politicians of all persuasion descended on Blackburn putting over their point of view. The great war time leader himself, Winston Churchill came, in an attempt to retain the two Blackburn constituency seats for the National Conservatives. On the night before the election, the town was electrified with an atmosphere of anticipation. The Labour Party with their two candidates staged ten minute rallies on street corners throughout the town, before descending on a packed market place, whilst the

Conservatives held their pre-election rally at King George's Hall. Finally after weeks of anticipation and suspense whilst the votes were being collected and counted, the result came in the form of a Labour Landslide, with a huge electoral majority. Blackburn returned two Labour MPs; John Edwards for Blackburn West and Barbara Castle representing the Blackburn East constituency for the first time.

Before the summer was out there was more rejoicing when news came through of the unconditional surrender of Japan, just two weeks short of the war entering its seventh year. With the prospect of prisoners of war returning home, a new government promising to create a land fit for heroes and an announcement that employment at the town's Philips plant was to be increased, it seemed that once more the people of Blackburn could again begin to live in hope of a better age to come.

EVENTS - SEPTEMBER 1939 - 1945.

1939
- 1,300 Children Evacuated from Manchester to Blackburn, (1-2 Sept).
- Blackburn Rovers play first home match since promotion to first division, (2 Sept), following week, league suspended.
- Chamberlain broadcasts to the nation, Declaration of war, (3 Sept).
- Former Blackburn man on torpedoed ship, *Athenia*.
- Friday market introduced in compensation for blackout.
- Blackburn man dies on torpedoed battleship, Royal Oak.

1940
- Coldest winter for many years, heavy snowfalls, (27/28/29 Jan).
- Blackburn Infirmary makes provisions for National Scheme of War Emergency Services.
- Clement Atlee outlines Labour's peace aims at *King George's Hall*.
- Dig for Victory campaign launched.
- Death of Rover's Manager and former player, Bob Crompton, club's longest serving player.
- A dozen mills remain in operation, engaged in government work, during the annual wakes week shutdown. Banks, offices and shops close for two days only.
- Emergency Committee decide Blackburn Blackout must be absolute, without even subdued lighting in the streets.
- Fire at Scotland Bank Mill.
- Henry Wood conducts *Halle Orchestra* at *King George's Hall*.
- Rover's beaten 1-0 in Wartime FA Cup Final.
- Launch of Blackburn Spitfire fund.
- Introduction of the Home Guard - Dad's Army.
- Removal of ornamental railings throughout the town for war purposes.
- Influenza hits the town - 50 deaths.
- Start of Sunday night, *Garrison's Theatre* at *King George's Hall*.
- Unemployment figures, lowest for twenty years.
- Bomb drops in *Ainsworth Street*, killing two.

1941
- Distribution of indoor, Morrison air-raid shelters.
- BBC broadcast *'Workers Playtime'* from Philips.

- Removal of bandstands at both *Corporation* and *Queen's Parks*.
- Darwen tram overturns at *Ewood*.
- First British Restaurant opened on *Mayson Street*.
- Visit of Home Secretary, Herbert Morrison.
- King George VI and Queen Elizabeth visit Blackburn.
- Wartime FA Cup final between Preston North End and Arsenal played at *Ewood Park*.

1942
- Blackburn's adopted cruiser, *HMS Naiad*, sunk in the Mediterranean.
- Weaving placed on the list of vital war work.
- Suspension of market due to bad weather.
- Visit of George Formby to promote paper salvage campaign.
- Bells of Blackburn Cathedral ring for the first time since 1940, in celebration of the Allied victory in Egypt.

1943
- Relaxing of Blackout restrictions on busy streets, 141 starlights installed.
- Italy unconditionally surrenders, flags fly high on public buildings throughout the town.
- New Pleasington Cemetery opened.
- First batch of local prisoners of war return home to Blackburn.
- Ringing of church bells resumed.
- Ballot votes against Sunday Cinema.

1944
- Cab man's shelter, Boulevard removed.
- Death of Major James Hawsley Gilbert Feilden of *Witton Park*, Lord of the Manor of Blackburn, aged 78.
- American GIs arrive in the town, in preparation for the invasion of Europe, accommodated at the disused *Brookhouse Mill*.
- Visit of Prince Berhard of the Netherlands.
- Allied invasion of Normandy, D-Day, (6 Jun).
- First batch of wounded soldiers arrive at the Royal Infirmary, (27 Jun).
- Proposed new town centre development plan published.

1945
- Schools closed due to severe cold weather.
- Shortage of coke places Blackburn's bakeries in difficult situation.
- Civic development committee, recommend the demolition of empty properties in the *Water Street/Old Chapel Street* areas in anticipation of town centre redevelopment.
- Coal shortages, Emergency committee discusses the possibility of some people having to do without.
- Death of noted violinist, E Romaine O'Malley of *Preston New Road*.
- Death of *Strong Dick*, alias, Richard Thompson, aged 77.
- Victory in Europe declared, celebrations throughout the town, (8 May).
- Visit of Prime Minister, Winston Churchill.
- Landslide victory for Labour in the first General Election in ten years, Blackburn returns two Labour MP's, John Edwards and *Barbara Castle*.
- Plan announced to extend Philips factory.
- Death of mill owner, William Birtwistle.
- £2 million extension at *Whitebirk Power Station* completed.
- Victory in Japan, brings the Second World War officially to an end, (15 Aug).

6. THE ROAD TO RECOVERY - 1946-1949.

IN THIS PERIOD OF PEACE DIRECTLY following the ending of the Second World War, the road to recovery seemed to be a long and almost endless trail. The news at this time became dominated with the Nürnberg war trials, sentencing Nazis for their crimes against humanity. Friction intensified between, the wartime allies USA and USSR, as the Cold War came about. There was the Berlin airlift and the birth of NATO. China became communist with the declaration of the People's Republic. The Jewish state of Israel came into being and the jewel in the British Empire, India, gained her independence. On the progress front, the new Morris Minor, the smaller family car was produced, the Land Rover was developed and the first jet-powered aircraft, the Comet, flew.

Despite the fact that the war was over, the sufferings of Blackburnians were not at an end as this new era arrived. In these monochrome years, the new Labour administration set about putting into action their scheme for revitalising the Country's sadly ailing infrastructure. For Blackburn this period saw the Whitebirk Electricity Generating Station taken under state control as were the town's hospitals with the formation of the National Health Service and railways in the area were integrated into a nationalised British Railways network. At a time when the welfare state came into being and the first family allowances were paid, the nation's birth rate exploded as the flow of soldiers returning from the war continued. Women returned to the home, their efforts greatly appreciated during the war, but such were the huge levels of labour shortages, especially in the textile industry, that immigrants were brought in from the Displaced Persons Camps of Eastern Europe: Lithuanians, Poles, Estonians, Latts and Ukrainians. Italians also came to help push industry to full production, to produce goods for export in order to pay off the huge debts incurred during the war, especially the lease-lend from the USA.

In this age of expectancy and of better things to come, anxious wives and mothers eagerly awaited the return of husbands and sons back from the war, with many a Blackburn street bedecked having flags, bunting and banners with welcome home messages strewn across them. Mill owners of those mills requisitioned during the war for Government purposes looked to a day when they could resume production once more. Girls with heads full of promises waited impatiently for calls from demobbed GIs to join them to start a new life in the States and a chance to leave this drab age of reconstruction behind, whilst for many there was the long awaited hope for a return to normality when rationing and tiresome restrictions would be at an end. But for others it was an age of great sadness, especially those wives and mothers whose loved ones were destined not to return.

Those who believed that there would be a rapid and sudden end to all the country's problems with the ending of the war, were in for a rude awakening in this post-war period. Rationing continued being further extended to include bread. For ladies prepared to take a chance and queue, there was the possibility of obtaining a pair of nylon stockings which trickled into some of the town's shops and bewildered children under the age of twelve were amongst the first to receive bananas, when a boatload docked in 1946, the first bunches to be seen in Blackburn's greengrocers shops since before the start of the war. It was also during 1946, that the death was announced of the 'Lady Bountiful', Mrs Elma Yerburgh formerly of Woodfold Hall, near Mellor, the daughter of the late Daniel Thwaites, who had generously donated so much money to provide for the town.

The ending of hostilities meant that at last the council was able to revive a number of projects suspended following the outbreak of war. A £258,000 order for buses was placed by the council as the scheme to replace the town's electric trams resumed with their withdrawal on the Preston New Road route. To ease housing problems a plan was approved to erect temporary houses in the Audley area and a programme to build 800 new houses in the following two years was agreed. After many years of negotiation, Blackburn Town Council finally secured a deal with Major General Randle Feilden, son of the

Witton House, home to the Feilden Family Lords of the Manor of Blackburn. The house and estate were purchased by Blackburn Borough Council during 1946. *Photo courtesy of Blackburn Library.*

late Major James Feilden, to purchase Witton House and the surrounding Park for £64,000, the last pieces of land owned by the Feilden family, finally ending the historic role of the Lord of the Manor of Blackburn.

As 1946 became 1947, the grim realisation that there was to be no swift metamorphosis in this post-war period was further highlighted as the coldest and bitterest winter since 1940 descended, a cruel blow to a town which had endured the very hardest of times, a winter which seemed to test the very limits of human endurance, but after six years of war, peoples resilience rallied once more in the face of the return of some of the worst aspects of the previous twenty-five years; the re-introduction of fuel rationing, power cuts and blackouts. 24,000 were temporarily unemployed in Blackburn owing to insufficient quantities of fuel available to power the town's mills and those who did have work to go to went about their business wrapped up in as much warm clothing as possible, often having to work in freezing conditions with only a candle for light. But this proved to be a final testing point for a town which had suffered over a quarter of a century of hardship for after this long cold winter of misery, there came spring, followed by one of the hottest summers on record, but in case people enjoyed themselves a little too much, there came the obligatory drought warning and the threat of water rationing. The sense of renewed hope carried on into that autumn,

The Market Hall 1948, celebrates it centenary. A hundred years earlier it had been the first public building to open in the town.

Photo courtesy of Blackburn Library.

further brightened by the marriage of Princess Elizabeth to Prince Philip of Greece; Blackburn's civic gift being a length of material woven on the town's looms. From this time onwards, it seemed that the wheels of progress after a seemingly endless dormant period were beginning to move into action once more.

Signs of recovery continued into 1948 and at last it looked as if the days were numbered for a never ending rout of make do and mend which had prevailed for so long. Blackburn Rovers suffered a set back being relegated to the second division of the Football League, the market hall celebrated its centenary, Queen Elizabeth visited Haston Lee Mill, child star Julie Andrews appeared at a British Legion Concert at King George's Hall and the Freedom of the Borough of Blackburn was conferred on the East Lancashire Regiment in grateful recognition of their efforts in the two world wars. In a year tinged with horror and sadness following the brutal murder of June Anne Devanney aged 3 years taken from her cot at Queen's Park Hospital, a mass finger printing campaign ensued throughout Blackburn and former Scots Guard, Peter Griffiths was hanged for his crime. The following year clothes rationing was withdrawn as the 'new look' in fashion was launched. With the ability to use more cloth in outfits, longer dresses and coats flowed into Blackburn's shops. Italian tenor Beniamino Gigli sang to an audience of 3,000 at King George's Hall, Gracie Fields visited and the Cathedral bells were re-

Wilpshire Bus Terminus, Salford Bridge. Buses had replaced trams on the Wilpshire route in 1947. On Good Fridays crowds would queue around the Bay Horse Hotel in Salford, for the annual outing to Ribchester and Sale Wheel Woods. The buildings behind the two buses stand in New Water Street which ran along the bank of the River Blakewater. On the left Woolworth's, the wall of which faces onto Holme Street. In the centre of the view is the Cinema Royal in Ainsworth Street. *Photo courtesy of Blackburn Library.*

A civic reception is held for the running of Blackburn's last electric tram in 1949 after a service lasting 50 years. The withdrawal of the trams would have taken place earlier, had it not been for the war and fuel restrictions. *Photo courtesy of Blackburn Library.*

dedicated following their recasting during 1949. This year also saw the final withdrawal of the town's trams, firstly on the Darwen route followed by a civic send-off for the last official tram service, a host of civic dignitaries taking their last tram ride in the Borough, from the Boulevard to the tram shed at Intack.

As the new decade approached, things finally were beginning to start to look rosier. For over 30 years, Blackburn and its population had had to endure some very difficult and lean years, but the town had survived, its weaving though greatly reduced over those years was still a sizable force, but had been joined by some other very valuable industries. Depression, War and reconstruction had by the end of 1949 more or less passed and as 1950 approached it was full steam ahead towards hopefully a more prosperous time. Little by little restrictions were being lifted and the lights of Blackburn were ready to shine once more.

Events 1946 - 1949.

1946
- Buses replace trams on *Preston New Road* route.
- Erection of 25 aluminium, prefab type houses at Audley.
- Defeat of vote allowing Sunday cinema.
- Blackburn Electricity Committee expresses itself in favour of State control.
- Programme to build 800 new houses in two years approved.
- Official civic victory celebrations, (21 Jun).
- Consecration of *St Alban's Church,* Councillor Sarah Buckley selected as first lady mayor of Blackburn.
- Diamond Jubilee of *St Barnabas Church.*
- Death at *Castle Douglas,* Dumfriesshire of Mrs Elma Yerburgh.
- Visit of Mrs Atlee opening branch of YWCA.
- Plaque unveiled in *Mill Lane* at the birth place of blind composer, W.Wolstenholme.
- £250,000 order placed for buses.
- Diamond Jubilee of *St Matthews Church.*
- The Rivers Darwen and Blakewater burst their banks, houses reached by boat in *Whalley Banks* area.
- Centenary of the Blackburn to *Preston Railway Line.*
- Blackburn town council acquire the house and estate of the Late JHG Feilden for £64,000.
- First payment of Family Allowance paid.
- Civic Welcome for returning Prisoners of War from the Far East.

1947
- Visit of Aneurin Bevan, Minister for Health.
- Clippies return to *Corporation transport.*
- Visit of the Princess Royal, (Princess Mary).
- Silver Jubilee of *St Saviours Church.*
- WE Moss of *Lees Hall* Mission becomes President of the *British Temperance League.*
- Heavy Snowfalls as coldest winter since 1940 begins.
- Coal shortages causes schools to close and mills to suspend production and power cuts imposed.
- 24,000 Temporarily unemployed due to fuel shortages
- Marriage of Princess Elizabeth to Prince Philip of Greece - Blackburn send material woven on local looms as civic gift.

1948
- Centenary of *Market Hall.*
- European Volunteers arrive to work the town's mill due to labour shortages.
- Golden Jubilee of *Feniscowles Methodist Church.*
- Peter Griffiths hanged at Walton Prison for the murder of June Anne Devanney at *Queen's Park Hospital.*
- Child star Julie Andrews appears at *King George's Hall.*
- Queen Elizabeth, visits Haston Lee Mill.
- Centenary of Mill Hill Congregational Church.
- Final meeting of the governing board of the Royal Infirmary prior to it passing under state control.
- Blackburn Rovers relegated to Division 2.
- Freedom of the Borough conferred on the Blackburn division of the East Lancs Regiment.
- Visit of Gracie Fields to *King George's Hall.*

1949
- Death of Father Fox, founder of *St Mary's RC College.*
- Buses replace trams on Darwen route.
- Centenary of the founding of *St Anne's RC Church.*
- Italian tenor, Beniamino Gigli, sings to an audience of 3,000 at *King George's Hall.*
- The last Blackburn Corporation tram makes its last journey to the Intack depot, being given a civic send off from the Boulevard.
- Cathedral Bells rededicated following recasting.

7. MIXED FORTUNES - 1950-1959.

THIS MAY HAVE BEEN THE FIRST FULL decade after the end of the Second World War, but peace during the 1950's seemed an elusive commodity, with the Korean War, the Suez Crises and Russia and the USA viewing one another with suspicion across the Baring Straits, as the nuclear arms race, accelerated. This was the decade when the world of popular music was turned upside down with the arrival of 'rock 'n' roll', fuelling the fires of teenage rebellion and together with a new genre of motion picture, new popular heroes were created: James Dean, Marlon Brando, Bridget Bardot, Marilyn Monroe and of course Elvis Presley. In Britain, the nation was plunged into a state of mourning with the unexpected death of George VI, brightened by the coronation sixteen months later of his elder daughter, crowned Queen Elizabeth II. Mount Everest was conquered, the four minute mile bettered, the water speed record broken, rationing finally came to an end and in this period of full employment, the Prime Minister told the population that they had never had it so good.

For Blackburn, the fifties became an era of calm between the storms of the Second World War of the Forties and the massive redevelopment the sixties would bring. In this age of mixed fortunes,

Salford and Church Street in 1950 after the withdrawal of the trams with the construction of a traffic island underway. *Photo courtesy of Blackburn Library.*

The Borough of Blackburn celebrates the centenary of the Charter of Incorporation in 1951, the Town Hall resplendent with flags and bunting to mark the occasion. *Photo courtesy of Blackburn Library.*

the Borough of Blackburn celebrated the centenary of the granting of the Charter of Incorporation by Queen Victoria, at a time a hundred years before, when the town was undergoing rapid change, a profound increase in population and greater town planning. During the month of August 1951, a programme of pageants, galas, sporting events, exhibitions and concerts were arranged to mark this milestone anniversary. At the end of this month, a fly past of the then world's largest airliner, Brabazon, casting a shadow on the town as it flew over, signalled the start of the Grand Centenary Parade, a procession of floats displaying the town's many trades, businesses and industries, demonstrating that over the previous twenty years there had been a shift from textiles into other areas of manufacture. By 1951, 25% of the town's population were employed in textiles as opposed to the 60% employed in the industry up to the start of the Great Depression, twenty-two years earlier, showing that at last heed had been taken of the Chamber of Commerce's statement of the town only 'having one string to their bow', Blackburn having learned its lesson the hard way.

Not unexpectedly, since the Charter of Incorporation had been granted at a time when the town was developing, other establishments celebrated a hundred years of influence in the town including the Town Hall, Corporation Park, the Blackburn to Chatburn Railway line, the Convent of the Sisters of Notre Dame at Brookhouse Lodge, the Infirmary and the town's highly respected weekly journal the Blackburn Times. The Easter Fair also celebrated the hundredth anniversary since its move from Blakey Moor to the Market Square, the latest attraction being Shaw's 'Hurricane Jets', a favourite ride for many a dad attempting to impress offsprings with their flying skills on this ground based attraction, just one of the many ways fathers found of spending time with their children and making up for lost time whilst they were away at war. Other anniversaries celebrated during the fifties included Blackburn Rovers 75th, St Silas's C of E Church's Golden Jubilee, whilst Thwaites's Brewery celebrated a 150 years as the town's brewer.

In the field of science and technology, there were favourable movements with the introduction of vaccines to protect against Poliomyelitis and Tuberculosis, both prevalent in populous places like Blackburn. The opening of the Holme Moss transmitter on moors near Sheffield enabled television pictures to be picked up in Blackburn for the first time, the televised funeral of the King followed by the coronation causing a surge in the sales of television sets in the town.

The new Queen herself made a first visit to the town in 1955, arriving to a civic reception outside the town hall in front of a host of civic dignitaries, before moving on to view the Mullard's plant at Little Harwood. Other visitors to Blackburn during the nineteen fifties included, The Princess Royal, Lady Baden Powell, Arthur Askey, Gracie Fields, American film star, Danny Kaye, a young Bob Monkhouse and the renowned Italian tenor Beniamino Gigli also visited as part of his farewell tour. Political visitors included, Aneurin Bevan, Clement Atlee, Anthony Eden and of course Barbara Castle,

Visit of Queen Elizabeth II, pictured here inspecting the Guard of Honour drawn from the East Lancashire Regiment and drawn up in King William Street. *Photo courtesy of Blackburn Library.*

who retained her Blackburn constituency seat throughout the decade. There was a welcome for three soldiers from the town, released from Korean Prisoner Of War camps and also for Blackburn man Fred Cooper, who achieved the highest placing, to that date of any British competitor in the shooting competition at the 1956 Melbourne Olympics.

In this age when rock and roll hit the town, 'Teddy Boys' appeared on the streets of Blackburn as the crazy beat began to captivate the town's younger generation and fearing it may cause public disorder, decadence and promote rebellion amongst teenagers, the film 'Rock Around the Clock' was banned from being shown in the town. As consumer spending rose to greater heights with new household gadgets filling shops and motor cars becoming a commodity within reach of many, the removal of the market to a site between Ainsworth Street and Penny Street resurfaced once more as the Civic Development Committee looked towards re-developing the town centre, but once again, the plan did not go-ahead at least during the fifties, the centre remaining more or less the same throughout.

However, plans that did go ahead at this time, included the extensions to the technical college on Feilden Street, the construction of a running and cycle track at Witton Park, the crematorium at Pleasington Cemetery, the workshop for the blind on Mill Hill Street, the new Littlewood's store on Church Street, four new secondary schools, the town's first two old age pensioners hostels and forty years after the foundation stone was first laid, St Peters RC Church at Mill Hill was finally completed. With buses having taken over from trams, the Boulevard was re-organised, with the construction of covered bus shelters and the removal of the Gladstone statue, being relocated outside the technical school in Blakey Moor and the private hospital at Beardswood Hall opened, administered by the Sisters of Our Lady of Compassion.

On a sombre note, two men from Blackburn were killed and a further 164 were injured when a bridge crossing the railway at Bury Railway Station collapsed as Rovers supporters were on their way to see a football match there. There was also the Brewery Street siege, where a domestic crises went out of control, 2 people being shot dead here, including a Detective Inspector who was posthumously awarded the Queen's Medal for bravery and the town's former MP Walter Smiles was one of the 128 people who drowned when the Princess Victoria, the Stranraer to Larne passenger ferry sank during

The *Golden Lion*, Church Street, a former coaching inn, demolished during the town centre modernisation which took place in 1955. *Photo courtesy of Blackburn Library.*

high winds which swept through the country. The nineteen fifties also saw the deaths of the town's premier soprano, Kathleen Ferrier, cinema pioneer Sagar J Mitchell, W.E.Moss of the Lees Hall Teetotal Mission, former Rovers, player William Townley who in 1890, became the first player ever to score a hatrick in an FA Cup Final and Blackburn born archeologist, Professor John Garstang, who discovered the lost city of Jericho during the 1930's.

The fifties also bade goodbye to some of the town's most historic establishments and structures including the premier hotel, the Old Bull and the former coaching inn from the days of stage-coach travel, the Golden Lion on Church Street where it was said a pillar marked the centre of Blackburn. Live entertainment came to an end in Blackburn with the closure and demolition of the town's last theatre, the Grand on Jubilee Street, the last show being an all local cast presentation entitled 'Blackburn Takes a (Final) Bow', the site earmarked for a new telephone exchange. Witton House, home to generations of Feildens was also demolished and after three attempts, the 312 feet chimney, the country's tallest chimneystack at the

Salford Bridge and the River Blakewater, from Water Street. *Photo courtesy of Blackburn Library.*

Corporation destructor, on Bennington Street was eventually felled.

A spate of mill closures from the mid-fifties saw a total of 16 mills close between 1955 and 1958, further exacerbated by the introduction of the Textiles Act in 1959, re-organising the industry's structure resulting in the closure of a further 17 mills in that one year alone. The town's cinemas also hit a rough patch following the introduction of a second television channel, crippling increases in entertainment tax and costly new developments in cinema. In an attempt to compete with television, 3D films were shown at the Majestic following a £5,000 conversion, followed by the first showing there of 'The Robe', the first film ever to be shot in the panoramic 'CinemaScope', wide screen format, shortly before the cinema was sold to the Essoldo group. After many attempts, a ballot voted in favour of permitting Sunday cinema, but it came too late for the New Central, Olympia, Palace, Savoy and Ritz (Kings Hall) all of which closed within a twelve-month period. With the arrival of rock 'n' roll came a revival in dancing. Mecca-Locarno acquired the former Olympia Cinema following its closure, transforming it into the highly popular Locarno Dance Hall and a ballroom at the White Bull Hotel on Church Street opened.

Blackburn Rovers returned to the first division during 1956 and things were shining bright for them as this decade was drawing to a close with the installation of the first set of floodlights at Ewood Park. The last years of the 50's saw the town struck by the Asian Flu epidemic which swept through the country and the introduction of the clean air act - certain areas of the town being designated smokeless zones in a bid to banish the smog and grime in the town. As the 1960's loomed, the once familiar haze that constantly hovered above the town began to disappear and things were looking better as the next decade approached.

EVENTS 1950 - 1959.

1950
- New Blakewater telephone exchange opens on *Mayson Street.*
- Fire at *Brookhouse Mill*
- Charter of Incorporation granted to Blackburn Round Table.
- Golden Jubilee of *St Silas's Church.*
- Centenary of *Notre Dame Convent.*
- Visit of Anthony Eden.
- Death of former Rovers player, William Townley who in 1890, became the first player to score a hatrick in a FA Cup Final.
- Demolition of the Old Bull Hotel, Church Street.
- Lord Derby unveils memorial at QEGS in memory of the 78 former students who lost their lives during the Second World War.

- Centenary of the opening of the Blackburn to Chatburn railway line.
- Barbara Castle retains seat in General Election, Ralph Asheton (Conservative), takes the Blackburn west seat from Labour.

1951
- Death of WE Moss of the *Lees Hall* Teetotal mission.
- Centenary of the granting of the Charter of Incorporation, creating the Borough of Blackburn, (28 Aug). A Host of events celebrate the Borough's centenary.
- Centenary concert by the *Halle Orchestra, King George's Hall,* conducted by Sir John Barbirolli.
- Production of Noel Coward's, *'Cavalcade', Community Theatre.*
- Open air performance of 'Merrie England', *Corporation Park.*
- Centenary Cotton Ball.
- Royal Lancashire Show, *Witton Park.*
- Exhibition Tennis at *Alexandra Meadows* with a team of international tennis stars led by Fred Perry.
- Centenary shopping festival.
- Brabazon, the largest airliner at the time flies over Blackburn, signalling the start of the centenary procession.
- Centenary cricket match at *Alexandra Meadow.*
- Holme Moss TV transmitter begins functioning.
- Fall in town's population by 16,000 in 20 years.

1952
- Death of King George VI, (Feb 6).
- Civic proclamation of the new Queen, Elizabeth II, read from the steps of the town hall by Mayor, Alderman Hare, (8 Feb).
- Visit of Gracie Fields.
- 2 Killed at Bury when rail bridge collapses.
- American film star, Danny Kaye appears at *King George's Hall.*
- Death of Blackburn film pioneer, Sagar J Mitchell.
- Gigli gives concert at *King George's Hall.*

1953
- Kathleen Ferrier receives MBE in New Year's Honours.
- First two old people's homes open in the town, at *West Bank* and *Hillside.*
- Approval of plan to establish workshop for the blind at *Mill Hill.*
- Closure of Blackburn's British Legion club due to lack of support.
- Arthur Askey opens Homes and Gardens exhibition.
- Mayor opens the town's first 3D Cinema at the renamed, *New Majestic, King William Street.*
- Visit of Mary, Princess Royal.
- Reports of two flying saucers over Blackburn.
- Death of Kathleen Ferrier, aged 41.
- First ER post box erected outside railway station.
- Town bedecked in buntings and flags in celebration of the coronation of Queen Elizabeth II.
- Death of former Blackburn MP, Walter D Smiles.

1954
- Large scale flooding, Salford.
- 'Blue Bird', built at Samlesbury for Donald Campbell for attempt to beat water speed record.
- Rationing ends after 14 years
- Demolition of *Witton House.*
- Poll Votes in favour of allowing Sunday Cinema.
- First CinemaScope film, *'The Robe',* shown at the *Majestic.*

1955
- Unveiling of town centre redevelopment scheme, with plan to move markets to a site between *Ainsworth* and *Penny Streets.*

- Renovation of Boulevard, removal of Gladstone Statue to Blakey Moor.
- Gigli visits Blackburn as part of farewell tour.
- *Majestic* Cinema sold to Essoldo.
- Visit of Queen Elizabeth II.
- Centenary of the *'Blackburn Times'*.
- Pleasington telephone exchange becomes automatic.
- Clement Atlee addresses meeting at Mullard's.
- Death of Blackburn VC Holder, James Pitt, aged 77.
- Blackburn cinemas open for the first time on a Sunday.

1956
- Blackburn takes part in BBC TV's *'Top Town'* talent competition, being beaten in semi final.
- Blackburn man, Fred Cooper gains highest placing of any other British Competitor in the shooting competitions at the *Melbourne Olympics.*
- Watch Committee ban the *Olympia* Cinema from showing the film *'Rock Around the Clock',* fearing public disorder amongst teenagers.
- Winter Hill ITV transmitter starts up as a second TV Channel goes on air.
- Carmelite Convent, *Meins Road* and the new *St Peter in Chains RC Church, Mill Hill* opened by Bishop Beck.
- Opening of the crematorium, *Pleasington Cemetery.*
- Closure of Blackburn's last theatre, *the Grand, Jubilee Street.*

1957
- Closure of the New *Central Cinema,* sold to Hargreaves Tobacco distributors.
- Death of Blackburn archeologist, Professor John Garstang.
- Centenary of the laying of *Corporation Park.*
- Closure of the *Olympia* Cinema, sold to Mecca-Locarno.
- Blackburn Hungarian Relief fund raises £8,000.
- Asian Flu epidemic sweeps through the town.
- Rialto Cinema acquired by *Rank-Odeon, Royal* and *Empire Cinemas* sold to Essoldo.
- 150th Anniversary of *Thwaites's Brewery.*
- Workshop for the blind opens, *Mill Hill.*
- *Savoy* and *Palace* Cinemas close down.

1958
- Introduction of first smokeless zones in compliance with the Clean Air Act.
- Closure of the *Ritz, (King's Hall)* Cinema, *Bank Top.*
- *Brewery Street* siege, two killed.
- £25,000 Floodlights turned on at *Ewood Park.*
- Centenary of the *Royal Infirmary.*
- *Witton Park Athletic* track opened.
- Demolition of the *Golden Lion* Public House, *Church Street.*
- Blackburn Rovers win promotion to the 1st Division.

1959
- Textile Act permanently closes 17 mills in 12 months.
- Luxury Ballroom opens at the *White Bull,* Salford.
- Blackburn's tallest chimney at the *Bennington Street* Destructor is finally felled after three attempts.
- Death of William Grimbaldeston, last of the town's VC Winners.
- Closure of *Pleasington Station* proposed.
- *Mecca-Locarno* Dance Hall opens, *St Peter Street.*
- Private Nursing Home opens at *Beardwood Hall,* by the Sisters of Our Lady of Compassion.
- Beecham Group take over Cephos Powders of *Shear Bank* Road.

8. ALL CHANGE FOR BLACKBURN - 1960-1969

IT WAS THE PACE OF CHANGE THAT made this decade so remarkable, a time which saw the emergence of youth culture and greater openness, of hippies and flower power. The whole world was brought to the brink of nuclear war with the Cuban crises, stunned by the assassination of President Kennedy, whilst in Great Britain the Conservative Government was rocked before falling with the Profumo scandal. There was the great train robbery, the Moors murders, the M1 killing and the abolition of the death penalty. The world of fashion saw skirt hems rise to an all-time high with the mini skirt. There were drainpipe trousers, caftans, long hair and unisex hairdressing salons and in this age of psychedelia, colour television

The Arndale Buildings and new Littlewood's Store in Church Street, products of the town centre redevelopment of the 1950's. *Photo courtesy of Blackburn Library.*

was introduced. The Beatles revolutionised pop music, the first batch of decimal coins hit the pocket, the Beeching plan severed rail links throughout the country, England won the World Cup and in the final year of the sixties, one man took a great leap for mankind when Neil Armstrong stepped onto the Moon.

For Blackburn, the start of the nineteen sixties carried on where the fifties ended, the first year of this most radical of decades coming into being with little ceremony with the sights and the aromas of the town familiar to generations, remaining pretty much unchanged. Some of the town's buildings had been extracted from rows of property with others rising in their place. The Littlewood's Store and Arndale Buildings adjacent to Woolworth's were products of the town's redevelopment of the fifties, slotting in where older buildings once stood, carrying on a old tradition in the town where rows of buildings were made of differing styles of architecture from different ages. The town's cotton industry was still a sizable force in 1960, although greatly reduced over the previous forty years, thirty mills operating in Blackburn at this time; the industry's chimneys still dominating the Blackburn skyline.

The first few months of 1960, were not a particularly remarkable period, although a note-worthy event at this time was the withdrawal of passenger trains on the Blackburn to Chorley line with the closure of the station off Livesey Branch Road at Feniscowles. At the same time, steam-hauled passenger trains were withdrawn on the Preston, Colne and Todmorden lines, being replaced by a fleet of diesel-powered multiple units, although the might of the steamer was still required to haul goods trains in the region. The town's cinemas suffered a temporary set-back with the closure of the Victoria, brought about by a partial collapse of the cinema, however a couple of months later projectors of the shut-down Palace whirred into action being reopened by new owners, Hutchinson's Cinemas, who reintroduced periodic live performances there for the first time in almost thirty years at a time when the other disused cinemas were reopening as Bingo Halls and supermarkets. Blackburn Rovers reached the final of the FA Cup; the event was wrapped up in controversy from start to finish with an unfair system of ticket allocation denying life-long supporters the chance to see the final. On the big day, the Rovers were defeated 3-0 with disheartened fans, feeling betrayed and turning their backs on a football team that many had supported so long. What should have been a joyous occasion marked a turning point for the club, sending this once noble team on a downward spiral with dwindling support at a time when the minimum wage in the sport was lifted which hit the Rovers who were unable to match the wages of the big city clubs and nothing but a miracle seemed able to stem the flow of the best players towards the bright lights of the big cities.

The 'Winds of change', Prime Minister Harold Macmillan spoke of sweeping through Africa, were also reaching hurricane levels in Blackburn during the early years of the sixties, the Council believing the time was ripe to put into action the long awaited redevelopment plan for the town centre in an attempt to sweep away the Blackburn of old, blackened by a century and a half of industrialisation and replacing it with symmetrical blocks of concrete and glass embellished with brown and white tiles. 1961, saw the publication of the 'Blue Print for the Future' document detailing Blackburn's future development plans. A radical schedule contained plans for traffic free pedestrianised areas and a modern shopping precinct with covered malls, built in three tiers, the lower for servicing, the middle for retailing and the upper tiers for car parking. Included in this plan was the removal of the market to a site between Ainsworth Street and Penny Street, a notion considered many times before. Once this had been completed an extensive redevelopment of Blackburn would begin, including the demolition of the old market house, Victoria Buildings, the Essoldo and Royal cinemas, the blocks incorporating Burton's and Marks and Spencer's, the Co-op Emporium on Northgate, Thwaites's Arcade and countless smaller shops lining the town's bustling shopping streets. In their place would rise a precinct, which it was hope would take Blackburn into the twenty-first century, comprising of over 100, shop units, a 60 bedroomed luxury hotel fronting Church Street, a civic centre and theatre, public houses, restaurants, a cinema, a ballroom and extensions to the town hall and Library, two of only a handful of buildings to be retained in the new Blackburn. Thousands of curious people attended an exhibition, with models of the plan displayed at the town's Art Gallery, many of those whose livelihoods would be in jeopardy should such a radical proposal be adhered to. A public enquiry followed, giving traders the opportunity to voice their objections, followed by a Royal Commission, recommending several adjustments to the original plan limiting the extent of the redevelopment area to just 14 acres instead of the 150 acre development planned.

There then followed a period of quiet, 1962 being a year of relative calm before the storm of upheaval which would ensue once the plans for the new Blackburn went into action. That year saw the redecorated Assembly Hall in the basement of the Public Halls emerge as the Windsor Hall, a smallpox scare erupt after two people from the town had been in contact with someone in Bradford who had contracted the disease and the Mill Hill Congregational Church, with its landmark clock tower at the end of New Chapel Street closed due to a fall in numbers attending services there, the site earmarked for industrial development. A protest rally was held at King George's Hall, following the ending of textile manufacture at the Primrose and Ewood Mills amid fears the industry was dying a slow death as a result of Government complacency by failing to peg the levels of cheaper foreign imports, the Electricity Board in Bridge

The mammoth task of culverting the River Blakewater at Salford, in preparation for the town centre redevelopment and banishing the river which gave the town its name, out of sight at the centre of town. At the left of the picture is Church Street and Woolworth's store in Holme Street, later becoming part of Ainsworth Street. The last remaining buildings in New Water Street are in the centre of the shot shortly to be demolished and the River Blakewater and the entrance to Salford Bridge can be seen to the right of the construction work. To the far right of the picture is the Cinema Royal, itself destined to become a casualty of Blackburn's redevelopment. *Photo courtesy of Blackburn Library.*

Street, moved into the technological age, installing the very latest in computers with the capability of producing over 3,000 bills per day and parts of Blackburn appeared in the gritty film 'A Kind of Loving', starring Alan Bates and Thora Hird.

1963 began with the coldest winter since 1947. Nicknamed the 'mini ice-age'; the Mayor launched an appeal to provide money to help the aged of the Borough during the coldest weather. As the cold snap continued, people in parts of Blackburn were forced to leave their homes for fear that gas bursts may occur due to frozen mains whilst others were without water as pipes froze only to be flooded once the thaw set in. Last orders were called at the Lord Nelson Public House in Salford for the last time before demolition men moved in during the first month of 1963. In this year of major developments, the town's skyline was dramatically altered by blocks of high-rise flats on a clearance site, where rows of terraced houses once stood, the foundations of the seven storey Infirmary extensions fronting Bolton Road, were laid and work was well under way on the new telephone exchange on Jubilee Street. It was also during 1963, that work began clearing the Blakewater site between Penny and Ainsworth Streets in preparation for the redevelopment of the town centre, with the loss of Merchant Street, Water Street, the eastern part of Cort Street, together with another Salford Bridge landmark, the 'Bay Horse'. The site cleared, the mammoth task to culvert the River Blakewater began, banishing it out of sight. Once accomplished, work could then begin to construct the new market with its huge market hall, futuristic looking convoluted roof and balcony cafés; a covered three-day market; a fish, game and poultry market and a covered walkway lined with shops, linking all parts of the market, shoppers no longer having to suffer the inconvenience of inclement weather. To the rear of the complex was the wholesale market and car park on top with direct access to all parts of the new market.

As the decade moved into 1964, brewers, Dutton's accepted an £8million take over bid by Whitbread's, the year that fellow brewers, Thwaites's announced plans to rebuild and modernise their Star Brewery. The last Easter Fair staged on the Market square opened that April, with all the familiar rides, taking up their usual positions for one last time, before moving onto a site away from the centre of town. The weaving industry suffered a further set back with the permanent closure of Parkside Mill, Fountains Mill, the Malvern Mill at Livesey and the Pioneer Mill at Mill Hill, the latter switching production from weaving to a revolutionary plastic meshing under

The Easter Fair in 1964 taken from Lord Street, being built up for the last time on the market square. All the familiar rides taking up their established positions for one last time including Collin's Waltzer in the foreground, Shaw's Dodg'ems to the right, with the frame of Shaws Moon Rockets in the centre and Shaw's Motorcycle Rally to the right.
Photo courtesy of Blackburn Library.

the trade name of 'Netlon'. The new telephone exchange opened introducing STD dialling to Blackburn, holiday makers returned home to flooded houses, after the wettest Blackburn Holiday week for many years and Barbara Castle was re-elected as the MP for Blackburn in that years General Election, becoming the first woman member of the Cabinet in ten years, taking up the post of Minister for Overseas development in Harold Wilson's first government. In these years of the swinging sixties, when the music charts were filled with the sounds of the Beatles, Cilla Black, Manfred Mann, The Searchers, Roy Orbison, the Rolling Stones and others, Blackburn pop group, the Four Pennies became the toast of the town when their self-penned single "Juliet", hit the number one position. Comprised

This photograph taken during the final days of the Market Hall and the brick paved market square, evokes the traditional market atmosphere so long a part of local life. *Photo courtesy of Blackburn Library.*

of Lionel Morton, Fritz Fryer, Mike Wilsh and Alan Buck, the four had a number of smaller hits before disbanding, Morton moving onto television's Play School, then going on to play the lead in the London production of the Lloyd-Webber - Rice musical, Jesus Christ Superstar. Of their smaller hits 'Until its time for you to go', received the recognition it deserved when a re-recorded version became a top 5 hit, seven years after the Pennies' version sung by rock and pop legend, Elvis Presley.

But whilst the younger generations where grooving to the latest happening sounds around and going to places like the Starlight Club at Little Harwood, councillors were preoccupied by matters concerning the redevelopment of the town centre. By the autumn of '64, the Blakewater site of the new market was nearing completion and time was drawing near for the moving of the market. In a year remembered as a starting point of a period of goodbyes for some of the town's familiar landmarks, this became a time to reflect, taking in the sights and the sounds of the biweekly outdoor market for a final

When time finally ran out for the Market Hall, the last landmark of old Blackburn, the clock tower, was unceremoniously demolished. *Photo courtesy of Blackburn Library.*

time, the market square, venue of the annual Easter Fair, a rallying ground for public meetings, with Victoria Buildings at the western fringe providing a podium from where many an orator would speak on Sunday evenings, preaching doctrines to the gathered crowds and the market square being also a showground for itinerant entertainers: Strong Dick and Owd Chipper being just two of these. A place of character and of historical significance, the market square formed the heart of Blackburn, a link with its pre-industrial past as a market centre providing provisions for surrounding communities, this cobbled area with its sights and sounds and smells filling the air whatever the weather remaining little changed in a hundred years.

The open market closed for the last time on 7 November 1964, reopening four days later at the new location. Almost instantaneously contractors began their quest of erasing Blackburn town centre of old, starting with the fine Italianate market hall and its campanile, once the symbol of Blackburn's proto-industrial past, becoming the recognised symbol of the Blackburn of old and all those other buildings both of architectural and historical note swept away in the name of progress. Hundreds witnessed the demolition of the clock tower with great sorrow, a last minute attempt to save this treasure failed and on the 30th December, time ran out for the clock as it came crashing to the ground, so that by the time the New Year of 1965 arrived, both Market Hall and clock tower were no more.

By the spring of 1965, work was well underway with phase I of the new shopping precinct as market stallholders were getting used to trade in new surroundings. At Easter, the first Fair away from the Market square opened on spare land off Birley Street in the shadow of the Larkhill blocks of flats, where showmen realised the difficulty of the event not being situated on solid land as this Easter proved to be one of the wettest on record. This coupled with the event being held away from the centre of town meant that takings were well down, despite the duration of the fair having been extended by three days. A storm of protest ensued from both showmen and fairgoers in respect of the ground conditions, resulting in the fair being moved to the much more suitable site on Ewood Car Park, the following year.

Blackburn hit the national news during the summer of 1965, when a teenage girl died from Poliomyelitis. A mass vaccination campaign of the town's population got under way, bringing the potential epidemic to a halt with a total of 19 people having contracted the disease. However warnings issued by the Minister of Health advising outsiders to keep away from Blackburn, had the effect of forcing hoteliers outside of the town to refuse to board anybody from

Blackburn. The situation also affected the Rovers whose home games at the start of the season were postponed and after a poor start to the season, the Rovers never really recovered, being relegated to the second division at the end of the season. By this time, the first part of the precinct was nearing completion as the first shops began to occupy some of the units. Both old and new names were amongst the first tenants, British Home Stores being one of the new names taking up residence next to EH Booth the grocers, transferring business from Victoria Buildings demolished that autumn and enabling the first phase of the precinct to be fully completed.

With shops filling the completed part of the precinct, contractors turned towards the quadrant of buildings facing the now obliterated market square on the eastern fringe, running along Ainsworth, Victoria and Cort Streets, containing some of Blackburn's notable and historic buildings: the Reform Club, home to Blackburn's Liberal movement, the Crown Hotel, the Market Hotel, a commercial establishment providing lodgings for those theatrical stars who played the town's theatres and music hall and the last in a line of the 'Royal' entertainment houses. Though scheduled for

A familiar sight in 1960s Blackburn, shops empy awaiting demolition. These in Victoria Buildings, King William Street, were demolished during 1966, enabling phase 1 of the precinct to be completed. *Photo courtesy of Blackburn Library.*

demolition in the preliminary plan, the Royal Commission did not approve the demolition of the Cinema Royal, however after keeping hold of the cinema for almost seven years Essoldo eventually sold the cinema to the council for £130,000. Five months later, bulldozers moved in bringing down the curtain on another piece of Blackburn's rich history. A worthy successor to the Theatre Royal, this entertainment house saw many of the greats, the roll of honour including: Mrs Dorothea Jordan, The Kendals, the Great Macready playing Macbeth, Wilson Barrett, Lillie Langtree, Florrie Forde, Charlie Chaplin, the great violinist Paganini, Vesta Tilley, Lottie Collins, Mrs Patrick Campbell, Sir Herbert Beerbohn Tree, the distinguished actor, Sir Henry Irving and many, many more. The emphasis was on variety from 1909 until cinema was first introduced to this venerable building during August 1931, replaced in 1938 by a brand new, up-to-date purpose built cinema, the last to be built in Blackburn. Built to last a hundred years at least, the screen saw many of the greats of the silver screen although the last presentation, 'The Family Way', was a more obscure, albeit star studded film whose credits included, Hayley Mills, Hywell Bennett and John Mills, with a musical score by Paul McCartney. After its last screening, the auditorium emptied for the last time for an establishment which had brought so much pleasure to generations of Blackburnians in the 180 years of its existence. The final structure had lasted but 29 years, barely an adolescent in the time-scale of a building, but it was a sad and significant loss all the same; almost two hundred years of history being swept away in a matter of days.

The introduction of breathalyser laws, a nation-wide outbreak of foot and mouth disease and colour television for Britain, were amongst the other news items in 1967. In this year of flower power, Queen Elizabeth's Grammar School celebrated its 400th anniversary and St. Augustine's RC Secondary school opened on Livesey Branch Road - classes and teachers being transferred from St Mary's School on Dean Street off Islington. In the Livesey area, huge housing developments were under way; the lands of the Lane House Farm and the Livesey New Inn forming the Welmar estate whilst the former land belonging to the Beechwood and Holly Tree houses also became vast housing estates. The town's ever-changing skyline was further altered by the rising up of the town hall tower block above the new shopping precinct and a cross and column structure was positioned on the cathedral extensions, lantern windows, as building work entered a thirtieth year without a clear end in sight for the completion of the annex. Blackburn Tech was in the running with colleges at Blackpool, Preston and Lancaster, but failing in their bid to gain an upgrade into Lancashire's third polytechnic, the coveted prize being awarded to the Harris College in Preston and on a more unusual note, a report of the conditions of the Borough's roads, pitted with potholes became one of the subjects of the Beatles' song 'A Day In The Life', appearing on the sublime, 'Sergeant Pepper' Album, released in this year.

The Queen and Duke of Edinburgh paid the town a second visit during 1968, observing the Borough's 'Operation Spring-clean', a scheme to restore some of the town's noteworthy structures back to their former glory, removing years of grime - Richmond Terrace and the old Town Hall's walls, given the works, as blackened walls were returned to their original colours. On the modernisation front, Larkhill Health Centre was opened, the 150 feet chimney at the star brewery felled enabling further modernisation to go-ahead and Radio One DJ, Simon Dee officially opened the 'Cavendish Club'

The White clinical look of the new Blackburn shopping precinct in 1969, a far cry from the buildings which occupied this area only five years before. *Photo courtesy of Blackburn Library.*

built above phase I of the shopping precinct. During the summer, steam enthusiasts bade a fond farewell to steam locomotives, the event marked by a visit of the steam locomotive 'Oliver Cromwell', the last official British Rail steam powered service, passing through Blackburn Station officially ending the age of steam power as the less romantic diesel powered locomotives took over their duties, these mighty iron horses being banished to the country's preserved lines and special excursions.

As the last year of the sixties arrived, the Lord Lieutenant of Lancashire, Lord Rhodes officially opened the new Town Hall Tower Block extensions, just one of the high-rise buildings which had appeared during this decade. Over the previous seven years or so the skyline of Blackburn had altered profoundly, the diminishing forest of slender chimney stacks joined by these square blocks towering above the town symbolising the changes which had taken place in the town during the 1960's. No more was this change more apparent than at the very heart of the town, with its new centrepiece, all weather shopping precinct. By the autumn of 1969, phase I was complete, phase II under way with a third phase in the pipeline. Away from the centre of town, improvement schemes were sweeping away rows of terraced houses formerly homes to countless cotton workers; their demolition being almost a testament of cottons failing influence on the town. Yet despite all these changes, redevelopment, clean up and forward planning, the sad truth was that by the end of this most progressive of decades, the influence of Blackburn was continuing to wane as the nineteen sixties ended.

EVENTS 1960 - 1969.

1960
- Closure of *Feniscowles* Railway Station.
- Introduction of diesel multiple units on Blackburn to Preston and Colne Lines.
- Decision taken to build cantilever stand at *Ewood Park*.
- Cinema ends at the Victoria as building collapses.
- Blackburn Rovers beaten 3-0 by Wolves in FA Cup Final.
- Palace Cinema reopens, amateurs bring back live entertainment to the building for the first time in 28 years.

1961
- Massive scheme to culvert the *River Blakewater* commences.
- Publication of Blackburn Town Centre redevelopment master plan.
- Over 1,000 people visit the Art Gallery to view a model of the proposed new town centre.
- Empress Ballroom and former *Savoy* Cinema served with ban for defying orders and opening as Bingo Halls.
- Witton Park Girls school opens.
- Closure of the *Roxy (Regent)* Cinema.
- Visit of Hugh Gaitskell.

1962
- Redecorated Assembly Hall at *King George's Hall* reopens as *Windsor Hall.*
- Flu epidemic hits town.
- Death of HV Minors co-founder of Cephos Powders.
- First computer installed at electricity board.
- Closure of the *Alexandra* and *Palladium* Cinemas.
- Protest meeting at *King George's Hall* against slow death of the town's cotton industry.
- Closure of *Ewood* and *Primrose Mills.*
- Closure of *Mill Hill Congregational Church.*

1963
- Coldest winter since 1947 strikes the town.
- Mayor launches appeal to help old people during the cold weather.
- Public Enquiry into town centre redevelopment plan opens.
- Leader of the Labour Party, Harold Wilson addresses meeting.
- Visit of the Duke of Edinburgh to open recently named King George V Playing Fields at *Pleasington.*
- School Children at *Mill Hill St Peters* return to the mill when they are accommodated at the disused *Primrose Mill,* whilst the school undergoes extensive alteration.
- ROF celebrate 25th anniversary of their Blackburn site.
- Co-op store opens at former *Palladium* Cinema, *Mill Hill.*

1964
- *Thwaites* announce plan to rebuild and modernise brewery.
- Last Easter Fair opens on Market place.
- *Four Pennies,* hit number one in pop charts with their song, *'Juliet'.*
- *Cherry Tree* School closes for the last time.
- Brewer's *Dutton's* accept £8 million take over by *Whitbread's.*
- Spain becomes one of the most popular holiday destinations for Blackburn holidaymakers.
- Annual wakes weeks holiday wettest for many years, with floods devastating the Waterfall area.
- Blackburn adopts STD dialling code with the opening of the new telephone exchange on *Jubilee Street.*
- Markets Committee recommend the *Denville St* area as the venue for the 1965 Easter Fair.
- Barbara Castle returned as Blackburn East MP with increased majority.
- Last open market held, (7 Nov).
- Alderman Eddie opens new market and pedestrian subways at Salford.
- Demolition of old market with clock tower being felled, (30 Dec).

1965
- Demolition of *Mill Hill* Congregational Church, New *Chapel Street.*
- Easter Fair opens at *Birley Street* site, *Larkhill.*
- Girl admitted to hospital with suspected meningitis, dies of poliomyelitis.
- Mass vaccination campaign to prevent the spread of Polio. In total 19 confirmed cases. Industry, trade and entertainment in the town suffer as a result.

1966
- Telephone House opens on *Duke Street.*
- Easter Fair moves to *Ewood* Car Park.
- Edith Railton becomes Mayor of Blackburn, daughter Madge Hindle, *Coronation Street's* Renee Roberts becomes Mayoress.
- First shop, Gas Showrooms opens in Phase I of the new shopping precinct.
- Grocers *EH Booth* open new supermarket in precinct, selling their old shop in Victoria Buildings for £135,000.
- Demolition of *Victoria Buildings, King William Street.*
- Death of Blackburn author, Dorothy Whipple.
- Essoldo sell Cinema Royal to council for £130,000.

1967
- 400th Anniversary of the foundation of *Queen Elizabeth's* Grammar School.
- Lord Derby opens new YMCA at the newly named *Edinburgh House, Shear Bank Road*.
- Demolition of *Reform Club, Crown* and *Market Hotels* and the *Cinema Royal*.
- Cross and column placed on Cathedral extensions.
- Blackburn publicans fear drop in takings due to the introduction of new breathalyser laws.
- St Augustine's RC School opens on Livesey Branch Road (St Bede's).
- Nationwide outbreak of foot and mouth disease strikes cattle at Hodern Farm, Near Feniscowles.
- Blackburn Tech in running with three other colleges in bid to gain upgrade into Lancashire's third polytechnic.

1968
- Sweeping secondary school reforms sees the amalgamation of the town's secondary schools.
- Death of Rev. Percy Mark Herbert, the first Bishop of Blackburn.
- Visit of the Duchess of Kent.
- Radio 1 DJ Simon Dee opens *Cavendish Club* over Precinct.
- Visit of the Queen and Duke of Edinburgh to observe the town's operation 'Spring Clean'.
- Death of Sister Josephine Swift, former Sister Superior at *Notre Dame Convent*.
- *Larkhill Health Centre* opens.
- *'Oliver Cromwell'*, the last steam train visits Blackburn on British Rail's last official steam train service.
- Clean up of the town hall begins removing a century of grime.
- Death of Richard Hodgson, former Water Polo star.

1969
- Blackburn Borough Police Force amalgamated with the Lancashire Constabulary.
- Blackburn *Bach Choir* win BBC Radio 3's International Choir Competition for the third year.
- Blackburn town councillor, Tom Taylor and ex-Trinity Church Vicar, Chad Varah awarded OBE's.
- On the tenth anniversary of it opening, *Mecca* rename the *Locarno* Dance Hall, *'The Golden Palms'*.
- Town hall tower block officially opened by Lord Lieutenant of Lancashire, Lord Rhodes.
- Retirement of Blackburn born BBC announcer and newsreader, Tom Naisby.
- Blackburn branch of the *Samaritans* opens, the organisation founded by Chad Varah.

9. Deceleration - 1970-1979

HOT ON THE TAIL OF THE SWINGING SIXTIES came the sizzling seventies, an age of flared trousers and wide ties, of afro perms and skin heads, of long hot summers and winters of discontent and news that the next ice age was a-coming. There was Concorde and the cod war, decimalisation and economic crises, strikes and the three-day working week and unemployment and inflation. The seventies became a decade dominated by hi-jacks and terrorist groups: the Basque separatists, the IRA, the Arab League and an Olympic Games where the feats of Mary Peters, Mark Spitz and Olga Corbutt were overshadowed by the murder of eleven Israeli athletes. The Beatles bid farewell as the world of popular music became dominated by Glam rock, punk rock, disco and Euro-pop and in the world of politics, Margaret Thatcher became Britain's first woman Prime Minister. It was the decade when the UK joined the Common Market and VAT was introduced. Lord Lucan and John Stonehouse disappeared and two Popes died in the space of two months. There was the Watergate scandal and the opening of spaghetti junction, whilst the toast of the racing world was a horse called Red Rum.

Anyone familiar with Blackburn who hadn't visited the town in ten years, would barely recognise the centre with its mass of white and brown tiles, the new stores and the obliteration of the old market blackened by smoke. During 1970, the go-ahead was given for the

The new precinct and town hall in King William Street, showing the clock tower and the levels of the multi-storey car park. *Photo courtesy of Blackburn Library.*

town to go radioactive in the form of the town's own radio station, BBC Radio Blackburn. In that year's General Election the town returned Barbara Castle as their MP for the eighth consecutive time, the Minister for Education, Margaret Thatcher visited Westholme School, the go-ahead was given for brewers Whitbread to build a brand new plant at Samlesbury, replacing their town centre site and the Cavendish Club fell victim to the country's revised gaming laws, having to close its casino.

Blackburn's weakening influence on the area was further highlighted when the White Paper on Local Government reorganisation was published at the beginning of 1971, downgrading the power of Blackburn Borough Council and handing over the management of civic affairs to the County Council in Preston. Blackburn fiercely fought the proposal which would reduce the borough to a second rate authority controlled from Preston. Together with Blackpool, Preston, Burnley and 20 other authorities, they presented their case against the reorganisation to Michael Hessletine at a special meeting at Lancaster University in the hope that they could force a U-turn on the proposal.

Decimalisation Day took place during February 1971, the changeover from the established lsd. going very smoothly thanks to an intensive education campaign organised by the Blackburn Chamber of Trade who made sure traders were well versed in the new currency. However, Blackburnians were not slow in realising that decimalisation actually increased prices in some cases by over 100%, as the 1d bus fare became 1p which actually was worth just short of two and a half old pennies and before the month was out there was uproar throughout the borough as rate payers experienced the biggest ever rate rise.

Unemployment figures released during this year showed there to be a large increase in the number of people unemployed in the town, making this figure the highest since the end of the war, the year loom manufacturers, Northrop announced 50 redundancies were to be made due to a fall in exports. More bad news came in the form of football hooliganism, when during a home tie with Bolton Wanderers, away supporters wreaked havoc in and around the town centre and preliminary census figures taken in this year recorded a fall for a fifth consecutive fall in the town's population.

As the second phase of the new precinct neared completion, contractors turned to the area mapped out for Phase III, land bounded by Lord Street to the north, Church Street to the south and Northgate to the west, upon which the ornate Thwaites Arcade

Thwaites' Arcade from Church Street prior to its demolition in 1971. This was to make way for the third phase of the new shopping precinct. It would be another six years before construction work would begin. *Photo courtesy of Blackburn Library.*

stood, with its glass covered walkway, lined with a number of small, select shops - some of the town's finest. Like the market house before it, protests went ignored and so another fine structure came crashing to the ground in an ignominious fashion. By that same summer, shops were beginning to occupy units in the second phase of the precinct. Tenants included already well established shops, such as Norweb moving from Darwen Street, the Co-op vacating the Emporium on Northgate, Boots the Chemists, leaving their Church Street shop and also a second sales floor for Woolworth's. The GPO left its Darwen Street building in order to be nearer the centre of town, which itself had the adverse effect on the traders of Darwen Street, since people no longer needed to wander that way to pick up pensions, family allowances and benefits, nor to pay their electricity bills at the electricity showrooms; and there began the decline of the Darwen Street area, once a thriving shopping area, starved of its lifelines and left to decay.

Things looked very bleak once 1972, got underway. Electricity workers went on strike blacking out the town during the first few months of the year, bringing a surge in candle sales - shops and businesses operating with candle light and a range of storm and gas lamps strung from normal light fittings, but in true Blackburn grit, it was, as always, business as usual. One established trader John Forbes Outfitter on Northgate, supplier of many a school uniform closed down and the Duke of Edinburgh visited Pleckgate school. The late summer brought the first of a number of waves of Ugandan Asian refugees, expelled from their adopted homeland by the volatile and somewhat impulsive leader, Idi Amin and the Empire Cinema at Ewood was bought by an Asian businessman to show films to the town's increasing Asian community which had been growing over the previous ten years. As Christmas approached, the night sky was illuminated by a spectacular blaze as the Cavendish club went up in flames and fearing the shell of the building might collapse, shops in the precinct below were forced to close, many of whose stocks had been damaged by water seeping through the ceilings.

During the first month of 1973, the Canal Foundry of Foster, Yates and Thoms closed after 138 years and Whitbread's (Dutton's), announced production of ale was to cease at the Salford Brewery site, moving the brewing process to the new Samlesbury plant. Westholme school celebrated its golden jubilee, the demolition began of the Blakey Moor landmark, St Paul's School, a compulsory purchase order was served on the Odeon Cinema and Barbara Castle opened the Road Safety training centre on Ewood Car Park. Radio Two DJ Jimmy Young, broadcast the 'J.Y.Prog' from King George's Hall and Blackburn Rovers suffered a major set-back in this year being relegated to the third division, for the first time in the club's history, just when the uneasy industrial and economic situation was beginning to take hold of the nation.

Inflation, strikes, rising unemployment and shortages were features of 1974, a year which saw the introduction of the three-day working week hitting the town's industries as petrol shortages caused queuing at petrol stations and people were asked to 'Save It!'. The local Government reorganisation act came in on April 1st, the former County Borough of Blackburn becoming the Borough of Blackburn with many of the borough's former services under the control of

County Hall in Preston. This new borough stretched as far south as Belmont, swallowing up Darwen in its wake, creating a friction between the two former boroughs, with the 'Darrener' fearing the loss of distinction. In honour of this unification, both Blackburn and Darwen's fine coats of arms were ditched in favour of a controversial modernistic design, comprising of little more than an angular dove in silhouette. The buses too were repainted, taking on a distinctive 'toytown' look combining the red of Darwen and the green of Blackburn, albeit different shades as the new union attempted to start a-fresh.

Three of the town's landmarks disappeared during the year, St George's Presbyterian Church, with its huge Spire on Preston New Road, the Queen's Hall Methodist Mission and the Odeon, formerly the Rialto Cinema on Penny Street - razed for the purpose of providing 'valuable', town centre land for office development, but by the time the site had been cleared, the economic recession was beginning to bite still deeper and such developments as the one planned for Penny Street were put on indefinite hold as were plans for the third phase of the shopping precinct. For the consumer, the year saw the price of food and household goods soar. Crisis in the Middle East produced further petrol shortages and increased prices, reflected in the steady increase of bus fares rising by 60%. Car parking prices were also increasing, up by 100%, adding to the ills of the economic crisis sweeping the nation at the time.

Things didn't look too great as 1975 dawned as the grip of the recession tightened still further, although New Year's sales were boosted following a rumour that the value of money was to fall. Blackburn Rovers celebrated their centenary during this year, which saw them gain promotion from the third division - a far cry from their glory days. During the previous fifteen years, this proud club had experienced some very difficult times ever since the FA Cup debacle of 1960 set the club on a very rocky road, nose-diving out of the first division in 1967, dropping into the third six years later and only the year before were in danger of plummeting towards the very depths of the football league. It was Gordon Lee who managed to instil stability and halt the free fall, reversing the downward trend in this the club's centenary year.

Two more of the town's cotton mills, the Alston and Albion Mills closed down throwing 400 people out of work at a time when a deputation from Blackburn travelled to London, descending on 10, Downing Street, calling for a cut in cheap foreign imports. A second demonstration later in the year called for a cut of at least 20% in an

The Albion Mill near Ewood, once one of many palaces of King Cotton. It eventually closed during 1975. Its once mighty chimney here seen being dismantled. *Photo courtesy of Blackburn Library.*

attempt to preserve Blackburn's remaining mills at a time when the nation was asked to decide whether or not Britain should remain in the Common Market. In Blackburn 64% of the electorate voted to remain within, a picture reflected throughout the country. The day of the country's first referendum was itself wet, but within days, after a particularly poor spell, the weather picked up and Blackburn was enjoying record breaking temperatures as the long hot summer of 1975 began.

The latter part of the year saw deadlock being reached over the routing of the proposed M65 East Lancashire Motorway and plans to construct the much needed inner ring road in Blackburn were put on hold to be reconsidered at a later date. The good weather of the summer continued into the autumn and into winter, with roses being in full bloom in the town's parks and gardens that Christmas, bringing an extra bit of colour to the town at a particularly dull time of year, the festive season itself being uncommonly mild at the time when cinema returned to the circle of the former Palace Theatre after internal alteration there.

In like a lion came 1976, as heavy rain and high wind swept through the town on the evening of January 1st. Within 48 hours, these tempestuous conditions brought power lines, telephone cables, streetlights and trees crashing to the ground, the wind and flood damage leaving the council with a colossal £40,000 bill!

The early part of the year saw the town's unemployment rise to 6.5%, 1.5% above the national average as the trade recession maintained its tight grip on the country's economy. One of the mildest winters on record continued into the spring with Easter being one of the driest and mildest for many a year, with Ewood Car Park, site of the town's annual Easter Fair, usually awash with puddles was uncharacteristically dusty. During the municipal elections of that May, two National Front Candidates were elected, one of these, John Kinsley-Read narrowly avoided going to prison following a court case resulting from a statement he made instructing people not to sell their homes to Asians. There followed a period of intermittent marches through the town, with warnings not to go near the town centre on those days, not that the townsfolk were particularly interested in the National Front's cause, since it transpired that the NF's demonstration was made up of people transported in from other towns and cities in the country to swell the ranks.

On a brighter note, the town was again in the national news, but for better reasons when Bolton's Beverley Isherwood won first place in the Miss England beauty competition, as Miss Blackburn, being pipped at the post at the Miss United Kingdom finals later in the year and failing to represent the nation in that year's Miss World. With temperatures once more rising, the second consecutive sweltering summer got under way, as each day, record high temperatures were being broken. The Borough Arms reopened after a closure of twenty-six years in a deal between Blackburn Council and brewers Bass, owners of the Legs o' Man pub in Darwen Street, following the decision to demolish this historic hostelry, to open up the Cathedral grounds.

By September, the consequences of two hot, dry summers were being felt with the imposition of hose pipe bans and further threats that stand-pipes were to be installed on street corners in an attempt to conserve the town's dwindling water supply, however before the situation became too desperate, down came the rains. September also saw St Johns Ambulance move to the former Lees Hall Teetotal mission and the cancellation of the annual elderly people's holiday at the Blackburn convalescent home near the sand dunes at Lytham St Anne's, later in the year being sold off by public auction.

Any hopes for a repeat of 1976's weather were dashed almost as soon as the New Year arrived, with heavy snow falls bringing the coldest weather since the big freeze of '63. This was the year the Queen celebrated her Silver Jubilee and on the night before the official Jubilee day, hundreds gathered at vantage points throughout Blackburn, to observe a string of beacons lit throughout the country, signalling the start of official celebrations. Scores of street parties, galas and field days were held in honour of the occasion creating a carnival atmosphere throughout the town marred only by coolish, showery weather. The Borough too entered into the spirit, decorating the centre of town with flags and bunting and streamers, having two of the town's buses number 52 and 77, painted red white and blue and school children throughout the borough received a commemorative first day cover from Mayor, Nan Bramley-Haworth.

Blackburn Cathedral also celebrated marking the fiftieth anniversary of the establishment of the diocese of Blackburn. In its jubilee year, the cathedral's extensions were finally completed after almost forty years. During the war, work had slowed but never stopped, although the original plan needed to be revised due to increasing costs. Thirty-nine years after the foundation stone was laid, Princess Alexandra attended the ceremony marking the final consecration of the cathedral.

The year also saw a fire at Blackburn Rovers destroy 400 seats, an asbestos scare at the R.O.F., following the diagnosis of 'asbestosis' in a war time worker who had been exposed to the deadly blue asbestos dust and the lower end of King William Street was closed off at its junction with Church Street, as Phase III of the shopping precinct finally got under way. In a year of yet more strikes, there was industrial action at Thwaites's Brewery, queues formed outside shops and supermarkets, due to shortages of bread as a result of the bakery workers strike and an unofficial strike by power workers blacked-out the town. Firemen were on strike when the night skies were lit up by a spectacular blaze, gutting the former Bank Top Foundry, taking soldiers operating the venerable green goddesses from bases in Blackburn, Blackpool, Preston and Burnley several hours to bring the inferno under control, believed to have been deliberately started.

Things were not much better during 1978, with increased vandalism, school-children creating havoc on school buses, football hooligans periodically rampaging through the centre of town and

The Cathedral extension with lantern tower, finally completed and rededicated during 1977, in a special service attended by Princess Alexandra. *Photo Tim Fernandez.*

gangs of school children attacking pupils of rival's schools.

The start of the year saw the town's fire crews call an end to their strike action, but as soon as one problem was solved others re-emerged in the form of petrol shortages and further bakery workers' strikes causing queues to form outside petrol stations and shops. The Community Theatre closed down and shops and pubs in the Northgate area closed their doors in anticipation of a National Front Rally at the Regency Hall, which turned out to be a failure due to the numbers having dwindled over the years, the meeting passing without incident. Marks and Spencer's extended their store onto land where the George and Dragon Public House in Northgate once stood, closing their lower sales floor in the basement, the Co-op store in Ainsworth Street opened a fourth sales floor and King George's Hall provided the venue for a virtually unknown American band, Blondie fronted by Debby Harry, just as their first British hit, 'Denis' was beginning to climb the charts catapulting the group towards superstardom. For the second year running the summer weather was appalling, television presenter Keith Chegwin entertained teenagers at a summer event at Corporation Park and Blackburn Councillor, Tom Taylor received a knighthood in recognition of his services in education.

But as the year of 1978 drew to a close, early snowfalls gave an indication of what was to come, the longest coldest winter for sixteen years, which coupled with the industrial strife hitting the town became known as the winter of discontent. The first heavy snowfall of 1979 started on New Years Day, causing disruptions to the football matches scheduled for that day, the end of which saw snowdrifts as high as seven feet tall in some places of the town. Throughout January, February and into March, the snows fell, making this the longest winter since 1963.

By Easter, Blackburn was enjoying the sunniest and warmest Easter weekend for many years, but by the end of that week, temperatures had once more dropped. May 5th was General Election day and the snows were still falling as voters visited polling stations. For the first time since 1945, Barbara Castle was not contesting the Blackburn seat, London Barrister Jack Straw taking over where Barbara Castle left off by holding the seat for Labour, though it was the Conservative Party which gained an overall majority, forming a Government under the leadership of Britain's first woman Prime Minister, Margaret Thatcher. But although Mrs Castle had retired from domestic politics, it wasn't the end of her political career, being selected to represent the Manchester North constituency, in the first ever Euro-elections a month later.

International superstar, Andy Williams entertained at King George's Hall in this year and Blackburn Rovers were once more experiencing a difficult time as the decade was drawing to a close. In the FA Cup competition, they were drawn against the invincible Liverpool, putting up a fine performance at Liverpool. Though being beaten 1-0, the result was a highly respectable score-line in the face of such a formidable opposition, but from that match onwards, the Rovers found themselves plummeting to the depths of the second division, being relegated for the second time in the club's history to the third division. As the new season began, things went from bad to worse, sinking in this league, before beginning to climb the league table in fine-style under the management of newly appointed player-manager, Howard Kendall.

The third phase of the precinct was drawing to a close in time for the Christmas season of 1979. Debenham's were the first store to open in this new wing, followed by stationers, WH Smith. The opening of this long awaited final phase was combined with bumper sales in the period running up to Christmas, the seventies for the town at least going out on a high note.

EVENTS 1970 - 1979.

1970
- Approval of plan to set up local radio station in the town, known as BBC Radio Blackburn.
- Lowering of electoral majority from 21 to 18
- Closure of *Ribble Paints, Red Cap.*
- Fire at *East Lancashire Coach Builders.*
- Re-election of Barbara Castle in General Election.
- Closure of *Regency Casino, Regent Street* following tough new gambling laws.
- Visit of Margaret Thatcher, Minister of Education to *Westholme School.*
- Go ahead given for *Whitbread* to build new brewery at Samlesbury.
- Visit of the Duke of Edinburgh.

1971
- Blackburn Borough Council, fiercely oppose White Paper on Local Government reorganisation, which would reduce the town to a second rate authority controlled by the County Council in Preston.
- D-Day, Decimalization Day taken in its stride in Blackburn.
- Scheme gets underway to refurbish the town's pre-war council houses.
- Highest rise in unemployment, since the war, 1,149 men out of work.
- International superstar, Eartha Kitt, stars at the Cavendish Club.
- Football hooliganism reaches Blackburn during Rovers home tie with Bolton.
- Blackburn, Preston, Blackpool, Burnley and 20 other authorities present case against local government reorganisation to Michael Heseletine at Lancaster University.
- Fall in export of looms results in 50 redundancies at Northrop.
- Demolition of Thwaites's Arcade.
- Barbara Castle opens discotheque beneath Library.
- Hot Chocolate is introduced in Blackburn's primary schools in response to the abolition of free school milk.
- Blackburn Rovers relegated to the 3rd Division of the Football League for the first time in the clubs history.

1972
- Candle sales in the town soar due to electricity workers' strike.
- National Front clinch council seat in St Matthews Ward.
- Council provides site for Gypsies at Ewood.
- Visit of the Duke of Edinburgh to Pleckgate School.
- Classic Cinemas acquire the Essoldo.
- The £650,000 Saxon Inn opens.
- Blackburn receives first batch of Ugandan refugees.
- Empire Cinema, bought by Asian businessman to show films to the town's growing Asian population.
- Closure of John Forbes outfitters, Northgate.
- Cavendish Club burns down.

1973

- Closure of the canal foundry of Foster, Yates and Thoms.
- Transfer of operations from Whitbread's Salford Brewery to Samlesbury begins.
- Jimmy Young broadcasts his radio two show from King George's Hall.
- Golden Jubilee of Westholme School.
- Publication of 1971 census, shows Blackburn's population to be falling faster than any town in the country.
- Barbara Castle opens road safety centre at Ewood.

1974

- Implementation of the 3 Day working week hits the town's industries.
- New library at Shadsworth centre opens.
- Last service held at St George's Presbyterian Church, Preston New Road, prior to demolition.
- Gordon Lee becomes manager of Blackburn Rovers.
- Car Parking charges double, 5p for one hour, 10p for two and 20p for up to four hours parking.
- Closure of St Peters C of E Church, followed by demolition due to dry rot.
- Closure and Demolition of the Odeon (Rialto) Cinema, Penny Street.
- Cavendish Club reopens after £250,000 refurbishment.
- Demolition of Queen's Hall Methodist Mission, Darwen Street.
- Plans announced for new Lancashire commercial radio station to be based in Blackburn.
- Bus fares rise by 60%.
- Barbara Castle was returned as town's MP in both the February and October, General Elections with her biggest electoral majority ever.
- Closure and demolition of St Philips Church, Witton.
- Zion Pentecostalists distribute leaflets outside the Classic Cinema, where the film 'The Exorcist' was being shown, warning of the film's contents.
- Saxon Inn destroyed by fire.
- Calls for sugar rationing due to shortages.
- Blackburn Rovers finish the 73/74 season in 13th position of Division 3, their lowest ever placing.
- Year ends with local dispute and bakers' strike.

1975

- Deputation from Blackburn march on Downing Street, calling for restrictions on Cotton Imports.
- Closure of the Albion and Alston Cotton Mills.
- Blackburn cotton workers join demonstration in London, calling for a 20% cut in imports to protect the domestic trade.
- Further increases in bus fares. Third rise in less than nine months.
- Blackburn Rovers celebrate centenary, winning the third division championship.
- Controversy over routing of the proposed M65 Motorway.
- Blackburn's desperately needed inner ring road, shelved until at least 1981.
- Blackburn's new central library, relocated at the former Co-op Emporium, Northgate officially opened by PM, Harold Wilson.
- Cinema returns to the circle of the former Palace Theatre.

1976

- Year begins with £40,000 of damage following high winds and flooding.
- Go-ahead given for the M65 to follow a route following the southern fringe of the town.
- After extensive refurbishment, Classic Cinema re-opens as 3 in 1 cinema.
- Miss Blackburn, Beverley Isherwood, becomes Miss England.
- Election of two National Front candidates in council elections.
- Borough Arms, Exchange Street reopens after 26 years.
- Demolition of the historic Legs o' Man (Monroe's), public House, Darwen Street.
- St Johns Ambulance move their headquarters to the former Lees Hall Teetotal Mission.
- Closure of the Blackburn Convalescent Home, St Anne's on Sea.

1977
- Heavy snowfall in town.
- All-night jubilation held at the Cathedral in celebration of the 50 anniversary of the establishment of the Diocese of Blackburn.
- Fire at Ewood Park destroys 200 seats.
- Asbestos scare at the ROF, wartime workers urged to seek urgent medical attention, following the diagnosis of 'asbestosis' in a former worker.
- Second attempt for city status ends in failure.
- Co-op announce plan to build a fourth sales floor on their Ainsworth Street Store.
- Barbara Castle announces intention to step down as Blackburn's MP at next General Election.
- Silver Jubilee of Queen Elizabeth II, celebrations marred by poor weather.
- London Barrister and former Students Union leader, Jack Straw selected as prospective parliamentary candidate to succeed Barbara Castle.
- Strike at Thwaites's Brewery.
- Leader of the Opposition, Margaret Thatcher visits Blackburn Rovers, becoming Honorary President.
- Bread Strikes cause queuing outside bakers' shops.
- Unofficial strikes by power workers result in power cuts.
- Firemen's strike, 'Green Goddesses', brought out manned by the Army.
- Princess Alexandra visits the town, attending the final consecration of Blackburn Cathedral.
- Blaze at Bank Top foundry lights up the night sky in the grip of the fireman's strike.

1978
- Petrol Shortages cause long queues at filling stations throughout the town.
- American band Blondie fronted by Debbie Harry play King George's Hall.
- Closure of the Community Theatre, Troy Street.
- Councillor Tom Taylor made life peer in recognition of his work in education.
- Approval of plan to demolish chimneys at Whitebirk Power Station.
- Former St John's Primary school converted to mosque.
- Closure of pubs and shops in the Northgate area due to National Front Rally in the centre of town.
- More queuing due to bread strikes.
- Introduction of the free weekly newspaper, 'The Blackburn Citizen'.

1979
- Barbara Castle selected to become Euro-MP candidate for the Manchester North Constituency.
- Cavendish Club renamed, 'Romeo and Juliets'.
- Jack Straw becomes MP for Blackburn.
- Blackburn Theatre Trust acquire the disused Empire Cinema, Ewood.
- Freedom of the borough conferred on Barbara Castle.
- Blackburn Festival gets under way.
- American superstar, Andy Williams appears at King George's Hall.
- Debenham's open, the first shop in the third and final phase of the shopping precinct.
- Rovers relegated to third division.
- Bumper Christmas sales boost confidence.

10. THE FIGHT FOR SURVIVAL - 1980-1989.

DESPITE THE FACT THAT THE BEGINNING of this decade experienced economic crisis, by the end of it, so many people had been given hope of a better future, yet overall, the eighties became an age associated with great disasters, the Hyde Park nail bomb, the Brighton Grand Hotel bomb, Einniskillen, Harrod's and many more, all the responsibility of the IRA. There were the many accidental disasters, at the Hysel Stadium in Belgium, Hillsborough, and the Bradford City Ground fire. There was the Clapham Common rail crash, the King's Cross underground station fire, the Manchester Airport fire, the Lockerbie air disaster and the Herald of Free Enterprise Ferry rolling over outside Zeebrugge. From an ecological point of view there was the poisonous exhalations killing thousands at Bophal, atomic disaster at Chernobyl and the Exxon Valdez which leaked millions of gallons of oil off Alaska. There was Tiananmen Square, the Falklands War, the Ethiopian famine, three million in the UK unemployed and of course the hurricane which wreaked havoc on south-east England. It was also the decade which saw the collapse of the Communist Bloc with Hungary, Poland, Bulgaria, and Romania pulling away from the strangle-hold of Russia and after over forty years Germany became a united country and the Berlin Wall came down.

Barely had the people of Blackburn had time to get used to this new decade than the town's dole queues began to rise at an alarming rate. In a year which saw national unemployment rise to a post-war record of 2.2 million and rising, Blackburn was struck with rationalisation policies, take-over bids, plant closures and technological change. By only the end of January 1980, 480 jobs had been lost, painting the same sombre picture throughout the rest of the year as the number of jobless in Blackburn grew higher and higher. Not surprisingly, the last traces of Blackburn's once proud cotton industry was hit, planing this once vast industry down to its very roots. 300 jobs went with the closure of Imperial Mill; Greenbank Mill closed, putting 306 out of work, 175 jobs went at Haston Lee Mill; 40 jobs were shed at Roe Lee Mills; 110 jobs were lost at Cicely Bridge Mill, with the closure of Blackburn's last spinning plant and 150 were made redundant at Waterfall Mill. In order to meet budget levels, cuts in staff were made at Netlon,

Donaghadee Carpets and as the run-down of Whitbread's Salford Brewery continued, a further 95 failed to join their colleagues at the replacement Samlesbury brewery. Sears, holding group of tufting manufacturers Edgar Pickering withdrew, the works being taken-over by Cobble, who made 330 redundant in the process. Cuts in the Government's defence budget meant the loss of 414 jobs at the town's Royal Ordnance Factory and 400 workers in the valve division at Mullard's lost their jobs as a result of technological innovation - the micro-chip rendering the radio valve obsolete. This grim start to the decade continued into the following year with figures published in January 1981 showing youth unemployment to have doubled over the previous twelve months with four out of five school leavers having no job to go to.

As a sign of these bleak times, one of the few developments which went ahead during 1981 was the construction of a new Job Centre on the corner of Northgate and Lord Street. In the grip of this latest recession, showmen reported their takings to be down at that year's Easter Pleasure and Pot Fair which became the last to be held on Ewood Car Park facing a very uncertain future and the Mayoral office also was subjected to calls for its abolition, by a radical element in the council. Street parties were held throughout the borough in celebration of the marriage of Prince Charles to Lady Diana Spencer, bringing a little brightness to the streets of Blackburn and other events which occurred in this year included, the desertion of the Rover's manager, Howard Kendall to Everton, the appointment of Bobby Saxton as his replacement, the acquisition of the Classic Cinema (Exchange Hall) by the Unit 4 cinemas group, undergoing yet another name-change in the process and the destruction by fire of the memorial organ at King George's Hall. For the first time since the close of the First World War, census returns recorded an increase in the town's population, augmented by the arrival of the Asian community during the seventies and whilst the National news was dominated by news of riots in Brixton and Toxteth, racial violence spread to the streets of Blackburn with several of the town centre's premises being fire-bombed.

As the recession continued into 1982, with no sign of it abating, a special advisory centre for the unemployed was opened in Blackburn as the number of those without work reached 8,000 and was continuing to rise almost daily. In this year of the Falklands crisis, 1,000 people took part in an anti-war demonstration, in response to the outbreak of this war. The Unit 4 (Star) Cinema at Little Harwood closed down, the Blackburn Times ceased production after

127 years as the town's weekly journal, the annual Easter Fair was banned from the town and Thwaites's Brewery celebrated 175 years as the town's brewer, just as landlords won the right to open their pubs until 11:00pm weekdays and beer sales began to fall as a result of the recession biting still deeper. A cut in consumer spending forced the Co-op store in Ainsworth Street to close its top two sales floors, C and A taking on the lease and the closure-threatened Woolworth's store won a reprieve, albeit temporarily due to an increase in sales over the Christmas shopping period.

Crowd violence once again hit the headlines after a clash between age-old rivals Blackburn Rovers and Burnley at Ewood Park during 1983, with 16 being injured as a result of being caught in the crossfire of debris being hurled from the stands. For the first time since 1973, Blackburn Council returned to labour control and in the year's General Election, Jack Straw retained his Blackburn constituency seat in the face of some very stiff competition. As Constituency Boundary changes had brought the rural districts into the constituency, traditional Tory areas. The Social Democratic Party, formed two years earlier and having secured a number of significant by-election victories, were proving in 1983 to be a force to be reckoned with, though only managing third place in Blackburn in these elections. The Easter Fair rolled back into town, being held on a clearance site off Barton Street, ironically its home prior to being moved to the Market Place in 1852, the land-mark cooling towers at the disused Whitebirk Power Station were felled and after a series of fundraising schemes, work began on the town's hospice for the

Thwaites Brewery brewing tower, which dominates the Blackburn skyline celebrated their 175th Anniversary in 1982. *Photo Tim Fernandez.*

The 'Big Wheel' and the 'Round Up' dominate the Easter Fair after its arrival at its new home on the car park at Witton Park. *Photo by the author.*

terminally ill at Park Lee Hospital.

As the New Year of 1984 arrived, Blackburn was cut off when heavy snowfall and freezing conditions, coupled with abandoned vehicles blocked all the major routes into the town. Once the spring arrived the weather improved and after a particularly dry spring, there followed a second consecutive, long, dry and glorious summer, followed by calls for water rationing and the threat of standpipes, but before the situation became too bad, the rains, not unexpectedly began to fall once more. On a favourable note, Blackburn Job Centre reported there to be a decline in the number of jobless in the town, further boosted by news that work was to begin developing a £5 million retail park on the site of the former Whitebirk Power Station and the green light was given by Minister of Transport, Lynda Chalker for the M65 motorway link making the area more accessible. The notorious Pickup Bank pop-festival rolled into town amid controversy regarding reports of the sale of drugs at the event and anti-nuclear protesters marched through the centre of town, campaigning for nuclear disarmament. The town centre Unit 4 (Exchange Hall) cinema became Blackburn's last cinema with the closure of the Palace cinema and bingo hall on the Boulevard and the last meeting was held at Blackburn's Greyhound Stadium off Gate Street, shortly before the stadium was demolished, the land having been sold for retailing purposes.

More job losses came in 1995 with a cut of 100 staff at the town hall and even more were threatened due to a prospective take-over bid of Matthew Brown's Lion Brewery by Scottish and Newcastle. A report published during the year revealed Blackburn to be one of the most deprived areas of Britain with over a third of those unemployed having been without work for over a year, whilst 12% had been jobless for three years or more. From a more favourable point of view, 300 new jobs were created when Tesco's Supermarket opened on the site of the former greyhound stadium and plans were passed for the building of a £3.75 million store for William Morrisons on the site of the former Whitbread (Duttons) Salford Brewery. After four unsettled years, agreement was reached between Blackburn Town Council and the Lancashire Section of the Showmen's Guild of Great Britain for the use of the Car Park for the annual Easter Fair at Witton Country Park and after six years the Park hosted the last Royal Lancashire Show. Plans were unveiled to re-vamp the Leeds and Liverpool canal and the Blackburn based snooker player, Dennis Taylor won the Snooker World Championship.

Lord Square - a now run down part of the sixties shopping precinct. *Photo Tim Fernandez.*

It was a bad start for Blackburn in 1986, with the closure of the Woolworth's store with the loss of 90 jobs and adding to the ills of the shopping precinct. The oldest phase had only been open twenty years, the newest part barely six, but what was to have been a radical departure in 1961 was fast becoming dated, tatty, flippantly compared to a large public toilet and more seriously dilapidated and dangerous with tiles falling off. During the mid-eighties, the town's once proud Boulevard was also looking rather unkempt and ignored and in a poor state of decay, which was of particular consternation, since for anyone visiting the town, this would be their first and possible lasting impression of Blackburn. Deregulation of the buses during 1986, hadn't helped matters, as bus companies preferred to use Ainsworth and Penny Streets as their main termini, largely shunning the Boulevard, once the envy of other towns, where both trains and buses converged. Since 1981, the printing offices of the Lancashire Evening Telegraph had been empty, following their move to new premises across the road in High Street. The former Palace Theatre on the south side of the Boulevard had been left to crumble away following its closure in 1984 and the transfer of operations of Whitbread's Brewery to Samlesbury had left the old brewery buildings standing empty, until the site was acquired by Morrisons, who cleared the site, together with the old printing offices, another of the town's architectural gems lost in the name of progress.

By 1987, the new Morrison Superstore was beginning to take shape, utilising a host of different architectural styles. Centre to the plan was the construction of a replica of the town's former market hall clock tower, however, the one which was eventually constructed, fell well below the noble clock tower which adorned King William Street. The Queen and the Duke of Edinburgh visited Queen Elizabeth's Grammar School this year to officially open a new building there, bearing her name, 420 years after the first Queen Elizabeth granted a Royal Charter for the establishment of the school. For the town's shopping centre, there seemed little chance of recovery as a second major store, the Co-op withdrew from the precinct, next door to the former Woolworth store which still lay empty, giving the Ainsworth Street and Church Street area, a very run-down look. More jobs were lost with the closure of the Crossfield bakery of confectioners Kenyon's, and the closure of their 60 shops throughout the town and there was a danger of further job losses when Scottish and Newcastle finally acquired Matthew Brown's Lion Brewery, with rumours that the brewery was to close.

Someone else who joined the jobless was Rovers' manager, Bobby Saxton who was replaced by Don Mackay, carrying on Saxton's success in the Full Members Cup by taking the Rovers to Wembley for the first time in 27 years and bringing home the trophy with their 1-0 defeat of Charlton Athletic. The success of the team continued in the 87/88 season, starting the season with a record number of consecutive wins, heading the league in fine style, but losing their lead over the months which followed. Though gaining a place in the play-offs, they were unceremoniously thwarted by a 6-1 defeat by

Crowds Assemble outside the town hall in King William Street to greet the Blackburn Rovers team, following their victory over Charlton Athletic in the final of the Full Members Cup at Wembley in 1987. *Photo courtesy Blackburn Library.*

Chelsea. Despite being denied a place in the first division at the time, Mackay did create an interest and a confidence in the club, by bringing some big names though coming to the end of their professional playing careers, who had the know-how and experience such as Ozzie Ardiles, Steve Archibald, Frank Stapleton and Kevin Moran. Aided by the intervention of steel merchant Jack Walker who injected financial means into the club to rebuild the Riverside stand, the disappointment and disillusionment which had lingered at the club for the best part of thirty years began to be replaced by the possibility that Rovers' good fortune could return once more.

In the closing weeks of 1988, demolition men moved into the huge Palace Theatre on the Boulevard which had stood empty, since its closure four years before. Formerly the flagship of the MacNaghten-Vaudeville music hall circuit, the theatre had been dogged by uncertainty for most of its life. First opened in December 1899, financial difficulties forced it to close six months later, being sold to MacNaghten in 1900. The Depression and talkies caused it close again in 1932, reopening four years later after extensive alteration as the town's second 'super cinema'. Closed yet again in 1957, it reopened as a cinema during 1960, became a bingo hall four years later and following internal alterations in 1975 became a combined cinema and bingo hall until its final closure. This time there was to be no reprieve as demolition contractors moved in to bring the house down for the very last time on this great entertainment house. It was planned to build a new shopping complex on the site, but the plan fell through, leaving the site surrounded with boards covered with fly-posters in several stages of being torn off and graffiti, improving nothing for the eye of the prospective visitor arriving at Blackburn Station.

Another of the town's buildings of note, architecturally flamboyant like the Palace Theatre and also subjected to, but surviving calls for its demolition, was the Victoria Building of the technical school, now

The Victoria Building home of the former Technical School, now known as Blackburn College, which survived calls for its demolition and celebrated it centenary in 1988. *Photo Tim Fernandez.*

called Blackburn College which celebrated its centenary. A hundred years before, the building had received Royal approval when the Prince and Princess of Wales, later King Edward VII and Queen Alexandra visited Blackburn, to lay the foundation stone of the college. A century on and the centenary received Royal patronage when the Prince of Wales, Prince Charles, visited to unveil a commemorative stone, marking its centenary, in close proximity to the one laid by his great, great grandfather a hundred years earlier.

For the second consecutive season, Blackburn Rovers failed in their bid to gain promotion to the first division of the football league, being beaten in the second leg of the play off final by Crystal Palace. This last year saw the town being subjected to all-night acid house parties becoming the leading acid house party venue in the country. One could be excused for thinking that the town had seen the best of times especially with the impression at the centre of town that the town was actually dying, but as Blackburn moved towards the last decade of the twentieth century, there became a feeling of hope for the town. The summer of 1989, was the hottest and sunniest since 1984 and as the eighties were drawing to a close, there was a hope that the sun would shine once more for Blackburn and that there would be a revival on the town's fortunes, but only time would tell whether this sense of hope evident at the end of 1989 would be justified.

EVENTS 1980 - 1989.

1980
- Heavy job losses during first two months of year, continue throughout this year.
- Closure of Imperial Mill.
- Royal Lancashire Show returns to Blackburn.
- After one season in the third, Rovers win promotion to Division 2.
- Mayoral chains stolen in Town Hall burglary.
- Closure of Blackburn's last spinning plant at the Cicely Bridge Cotton Works.

1981
- Blackburn's unemployment rate 1.2% higher than national average.
- Report 4 out of 5 school leavers have no jobs to go to.
- Racial riots hits the streets of Blackburn in the same week as the Toxteth and Brixton riots.
- Street parties held in celebration of the marriage of the Prince of Wales to Lady Diana Spencer.
- Move by militants to scrap the mayoral office in Blackburn fails.
- Unit 4 cinemas take control of the Classic.
- Last Easter Pleasure and Pot Fair held on Ewood Car Park.
- Howard Kendall, Rovers' manager leaves for Everton FC.

- Closure of Court School of Dancing, above Burton's men's outfitters.
- Census figures reveal the first rise in the towns population since 1914, population 106,501.
- Fire at King George's Hall damages £350,000 memorial organ.
- Radio Blackburn renamed Radio Lancashire.

1982
- As unemployment figures in the town reach 8,000, centre for the unemployed is opened.
- Annual Easter Fair, banned by council.
- Closure of the Unit 4 (Star) Cinema, Little Harwood.
- Thwaites's Brewery celebrates 175th anniversary.
- Outbreak of Falklands War, 1,200 people take part in anti-war demonstration through the centre of town.
- After 127 years The Blackburn Times ceases production.
- Former Northrop works hit by fire.
- Shoe magnate Tommy Ball fined for Sunday trading.
- Mullard's make last radio valve as the valve division closes, due to the micro-chip.
- Pubs allowed to remain open until 11pm weekdays.
- Death of Miss Emily Hilda Singleton founder of Westholme School for Girls.

1983
- Work begins on the town's hospice for the terminally ill at Park Lee Hospital.
- Culture Club with Boy George play King George's Hall.
- Closure of the Cicely Bridge Cotton Mill.
- Blackburn Council returns to Labour Control.
- Whitebirk Power Station cooling towers felled.
- Visit of Diana, Princess of Wales.
- BBC's Antique Road Show Rolls into town.
- Blackburn Rovers experiment with Sunday matches to below average crowds.
- Annual Easter Fair returns to town, held on a clearance site off Barton Street.
- Worst ever crowd violence at Ewood Park following league tie with Burnley.

1984
- Poor start to year with gales, snow, flooding and freezing conditions.
- Report indicates increases in drug and solvent abuse in Blackburn.
- £100,000 Blaze at Ewood Park.
- Controversial Pickup Bank Pop Festival takes place.
- Muslim school for girls opens.
- £5 million retail park on site of the Whitebirk Power Station gets go-ahead.
- Closure of the Palace Cinema and Bingo Hall.
- Demolition of the former Northern Daily/Lancashire Evening Telegraph Printing offices.
- Fall in town's jobless figures.
- Athlete Shirley Strong opens the new all-weather running surface at Witton Park.
- Anti-nuclear protestors march through the centre of Blackburn.
- Closure of the Greyhound Stadium, Gate Street.
- Labour leaders in Blackburn celebrate the expulsion of 6 'militant tendency' supporters.

1985
- Approval of scheme to set up business park at Greenbank.
- Investigate reports 1/3rd of the town's births are to women from overseas places.
- Brewers, Matthew Brown, prevent take over by Scottish and Newcastle.

- Tesco Supermarket opens on site of former Greyhound stadium.
- Annual Easter Fair finds a new home at Witton Park.
- Blackburn's snooker professional, Dennis Taylor wins World Snooker Final.
- Visit of the Duke of Edinburgh to Richardson House.
- Report reveals the town's biggest tourist attraction is Tommy Balls.
- Closure of 70 year old Riverside stand at Ewood Park.
- Royal Lancashire Show held at Witton Park.

1986
- Closure of Woolworth's Store 60 years after being established in Blackburn.
- Demolition of the former Salford Brewery.
- Waves Water fun centre, Blakey Moor opens.
- Tommy Balls sells major part of shoe business.
- Centenary of the Lancashire Evening Telegraph, marked by a visit by Princess Anne.

1987
- Brewer's Scottish and Newcastle gain control of Matthew Brown.
- Visit of the Queen and Duke of Edinburgh, opening a new wing 450 years after Elizabeth I granted charter.
- Blackburn Rovers win Full Members Cup at Wembley.
- Closure of Kenyon's Bakery, Crossfield Street.

1988
- Centenary of the laying of the foundation stone at Blackburn Technical College marked by visit of the Prince of Wales.
- Death of Blackburn born entertainer, Russell Harty.
- Carl Fogarty wins Fomula 1 Motorcycle Championship.
- Scanner installed at the Royal Infirmary after £500,000 is raised by scanner appeal fund.
- Rovers denied promotion to Division 1 after being beaten 6-1 by Chelsea in Division 2 play-offs

1989
- Fire at Court House, King Street.
- Rovers fail in bid to gain promotion to Division 1 for second time in play off finals.
- Blackburn becomes national centre for acid house parties as hundreds descend on the town at secret locations.
- Visit of the Prince of Wales.
- Hottest July for five years.

11. - REVIVAL 1990 -1999

AS THE LAST DECADE OF THE TWENTIETH century arrived, world peace still seemed to be an elusive commodity. At the turn of the century, the Balkans were considered to be the 'tinder box of Europe', and over ninety years later sparks are still flying is this volatile region of Europe, with the states of the former Yugoslavia, Serbia, Bosnia, Croatia and Kosovo, still battling it out with all the horrors of twentieth century warfare: the refugees, famine, displaced persons, 'ethnic cleansing' and genocide. This decade has seen the Gulf war and the effects of the pollution in the aftermath; trouble in the former colonies of Africa and the eternal problem of Northern Ireland still smoulders, despite the Good Friday agreement. In a hundred years the world has seen political extremes from communism on the left to fascism at the extreme right, yet as we move towards 2000, the political pendulum has seemingly come to rest towards the centre-ground of social democracy. Despite, their persuasions, Politicians are still installing unpopular measures, whilst making empty pledges. We have been promised the 'green shoots of recovery' and told of the 'feel good factor', whilst introducing the poll tax and VAT on fuel bills. The money in our pockets has grown smaller with the introduction of the new 5, 10 and 50 pence coins and almost daily our national news has been dominated by the much-publicised 'Millennium Dome' in Greenwich. In this last decade, technology has continued to increase at a frighteningly fast rate, with the world-wide-web, e-mail, pocket-sized computers and shops which never close, yet the forces of nature still have the power to influence us all, as the last total eclipse of this millennium over a cloud covered south-west England and the partiality over the rest of Britain had the effect of bringing the country to a stand-still. Not unexpectedly as the year 2000 loomed, there were the age-old predictions of doom and gloom and the reminders of the prophecies of Nostradamus and of the world's end. Yet in a curious way, it could have happened, but not in the Armageddon sort of way prophesised for centuries, but as a result of the 'millennium bug' with the potential of crippling the communications, network and power sources, blacking out the world. All eyes were on Australia as the clock struck midnight there, but the hour passed with no such problems and the world continued as before with spectacular

A ghost from Blackburn's once illustrious industrial past 'Hawkin's for Cottons' still displayed on the Waterfall Mill. Weaving finally ended at the mill in 1993; the building then being split into small industrial units.
Photo Tim Fernandez.

firework displays welcoming in the long-awaited year 2000.

The arrival of this decade, for once, was greeted in Blackburn with a certain sense of optimism and enthusiasm and hope for the future, replacing the despair which had lingered for so many years. Not only did the nineties become an era of looking and moving forwards, but it was also a time for looking back over the last hundred years. Inevitably, there are the comparisons between the Blackburn of 1900 and the Blackburn of 2000 and those profound changes that the century has brought to the town. A hundred years ago, the decline of Blackburn's cotton industry would have been incomprehensible and the chances of a town so reliant on this one industry surviving without it would not have been believable. Though from the 1920's onwards mill closures became a common occurrence, which only slowed as the number of mills operating dwindled, it did not detract from one of the saddest events of the 1990's for Blackburn, when with the closure of the weaving sheds at Waterfall Mill; a particularly poignant piece of news, signalled the ending of the town's 150 year association with the once large William Birtwistle Allied Mills empire. Following the mill's closure the mill chimney, which had dominated Mill Hill for almost a century, one of the last survivors and symbol of Blackburn's cotton industry, was dismantled brick by brick. Almost as a sign of respect of the passing of this once great dynasty in the world of Blackburn's cotton trade, other former cotton mill chimneys bowed their heads as the stacks at the Eclipse Mill at Feniscowles, the Salisbury Mill, Ewood and the Malvern Mill at Livesey, all came tumbling down in this period, leaving very few examples of a structure which had dominated the skyline of Blackburn a hundred years ago. In the Blackburn of 2000, it is possible to find a weaving mill, but you need to look hard, in complete contrast to the situation at the beginning of this century, when weaving was everywhere and everything for Blackburn.

Despite the demise of the cotton industry, the town has shown that it has the ability to survive and in the last nine years there have been definite signs of revival. At long last, Blackburn could begin to move on and progress, although for the first couple of years, the town was beset with the same dashed hopes of big ideas and ambitious development schemes which failed to come to fruition, including a bid to gain city status in celebration of the fortieth anniversary of the Queen's accession in 1992. However strangely enough, after this set-back, good fortune did begin to come the town's way, starting with Blackburn Rovers, who after reaching the second division play-offs in three out of four seasons, finally gained promotion after an exciting play-off final at Wembley, during May 1992. From that day forward, Blackburn started to reap the awards of years of hard work, planning and perseverance. During the latter part of 1992, the council secured a £35 million grant under the City Challenge scheme to spend on refurbishing and redeveloping the more dilapidated areas of the Borough, preparing the town for the twenty first century and the new millennium and putting a sense of pride back into this run-down town. Interest in Blackburn was running at a new high with enquiries being made about empty units at the town's established industrial estates by prospective employers, in close proximity to the new M65 motorway which opened at the end of 1997, giving greater access to the town. 1999 saw the drawing up of an action plan to improve communications in and around the centre of town, aided by a £2.5 million grant from the European Development Fund, with more money expected over the following four years. At the centre of town, plans have already been approved for the building of a multiplex cinema behind the railway station. Here too, redevelopment is under way, the old Victorian train sheds are in the process of being demolished, to be replaced with a state-of-the-art railway station, complete with its own 'millennium dome', albeit on a much smaller scale than the one in the capital. Plans are also under discussion for the construction of a quality hotel in the proximity of the town centre, in addition to the development of further retail units in the Lower Audley area of town, near to the Ice Arena and Town's Moor Retail Park, products of the earlier part of the decade, all boosting the jobs, market as Blackburn pulls away from its somewhat grime ridden image brought about by its now almost non-existent textile trade. But even here, the old mills are being put to other good uses, though externally still providing us with a reminder of our industrial heritage. In April 1998, Blackburn with neighbour Darwen pulled away from Lancashire County Council control to become a unitary authority. Once again the town is in control of its own destiny, independent of County Hall in Preston and is now able to channel resources back into the town rather than having to deposit a huge amount of revenue in a general Lancashire County fund. As a consequence Blackburn is becoming a leader once more and has also become a role model, for other authorities in the country.

In anticipation of its new unitary status, the once crumbling town hall tower block, underwent the 'full metal jacket' treatment, with a coat of cladding and reinforcements being built around the structure, giving the town centre a new dynamic-looking centre-piece. During the latter months of 1994, work commenced on the revamping of the shopping precinct, which lay at the foot of the tower block, one of the schemes which formed part of the city challenge bid. Money was also set aside for the refurbishment of King George's Hall and the Boulevard's timely facelift, which involved an intensive clean-up of another key, but run-down area of town. The twentieth century extensions to the Cathedral were also in need of urgent attention, following the discovery that the structure was crumbling and so a fund was established during 1996 to provide money for repairs to the landmark lantern tower. A new set of stained glass windows were installed as a result, giving a kaleidoscope effect when viewed from below, rededicated by Princess Anne following completion during the summer, in time for the Cathedral to celebrate the dawning of the new millennium.

With grants and investments beginning to pour into the town, coupled with the rejuvenation and revival schemes, the council once more set their sights on gaining city status. In the Autumn of 1998, the Home Office announced that there were to be two new cities created in the next three years, the first in recognition of the millennium and the second in commemoration of the Queen's Golden Jubilee in 2002. As it stands, Blackburn is one of only two places in Great Britain with a Cathedral that is not a city. Those earlier failures might have been due to the fact that the conditions

Salford Bridge and Railway Road looking towards the Railway Station on the Boulevard. *Photo Tim Fernandez.*

were not perhaps quite right for Blackburn to be upgraded. In 1934, Blackburn was in the grip of the Great Depression and cotton floundering. In 1977, the town was in free fall to recession, having just got over one bout and in 1992, although the signs were more favourable, they still were not convincing enough to persuade the

Home Office, that the start of the boom in the town was more than a brief, short-lived, boom. However, in the years which followed 1992, the town has demonstrated, that the signs of recovery were indeed correct as there has followed a period of greater prosperity for the town. The Rovers' previous success has done a lot to put the town back on the map and in a town once synonymous with Barbara Castle, her successor Jack Straw has made his own mark, giving the town a higher profile nationally. All of these factors must be taken into consideration and yield a satisfactory outcome, for the time for Blackburn to become a city has never been better and would be a fitting prize should Blackburn emerge at the opening of the twenty-first century as the 'Millennium city', just in time to celebrate the 150th anniversary of the creating of the Borough of Blackburn in 2001 and should that attempt fail, there is also another chance to gain city status in the golden jubilee year of 2002.

Even though the last one hundred years has seen Blackburn lose a great deal of its heritage, buildings of note, and traditions in the name of progress, it still retains some notable institutions that were present at the end of the last century. The old town hall, Corporation Park, complete with memorial gardens dedicated to the dead of this century's two world wars, both celebrating 150th anniversaries in the first decade of the twenty-first century. St John's Church and the Hornby House in King Street, are survivors from the eighteenth

The Cathedral, one of the very few structures in Blackburn which can lay claim to continuous use for the same purposes throughout the 20th century and beyond. *Photo Tim Fernandez.*

century. The Museum and Art Gallery, the free library, the Grammar School and the Technical College, rescued from demolition, to name but a few, which were there in 1900, as was the Cotton Exchange Hall of 1863 still exist. Even at the end of the last century, the Exchange was periodically exhibiting moving picture shows, becoming the town centre's first permanent nightly cinema in 1908 and the only cinema in 1984, outlasting its perhaps more prestigious rivals, the 'super cinemas' - the Rialto (Odeon), the Royal and the Palace. During 1993, in line with the apparent 1990's policy of revival, it too underwent extensive refurbishment, emerging as the 'Apollo', a five-screened cinema under one roof. 1996 marked the centenary of British cinema and in celebration, the cinema screened a short season of classic films from yesteryear, some of which had premiered at this cinema many years before, in the days of it being the 'Majestic'. Into 1999 and having undergone five name changes, the Apollo is still 'packing them in', thrilling audiences with the very latest blockbusters with their ever-more complex cinematographic

Salford in 2000 is still a busy and major junction. Below the level of the road flows the River Blakewater banished out of sight. On the far side stands the White Bull, a former coaching inn dating from the age of stage coach travel. In a hundred years little, in this view has altered, except the pace of life. *Photo Tim Fernandez.*

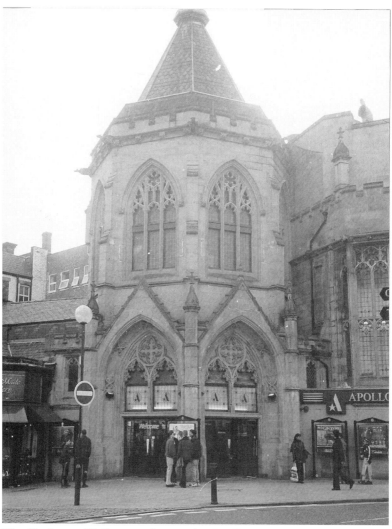

The Exchange Hall, operating as the Apollo 5 Cinema. Back in 1900, periodic film shows were held in this building. A hundred years later and it is the town's last remaining memorial of the golden age of cinema, having operated over the century as the Exchange, Majestic, Essoldo (and ABC), Classic and Unit 4 cinemas. *Photo Tim Fernandez.*

techniques. How many other places in Britain in this age of the 'multiplex' have an original picture hall of the 1900's still in operation?

The town's historic role as a market centre is still with us, although the new market of 1964, provides shoppers with a different experience these days, with it being undercover, than in those days of the outdoor stalls. The refurbishment of the new markets' complex during 1994 was completed in time for the thirtieth anniversary of the market's move, as work began to re-vamp the badly dilapidated and sadly dated shopping precinct. When built in the late sixties it was heralded as being built to a design which would take the town into the year 2000, but has since shown how fast the modern dates over the traditional. A mask of cladding was placed over the structure, banishing the white and brown tiles, following a similar Italianate style, that the old market house had been built in, nearly 150 years before. The new clock tower was also given the treatment, becoming the symbol of the new look Blackburn, in much the same way that the old campanile was the symbol of the Blackburn of old.

Blackburn Rovers still remain a firm favourite with the town's football supporters, despite the set back of relegation at the close of the 1998/99 season. The century's ups and downs could be said to

King William Street. By the mid 1990's the town centre shopping precinct began to emulate an italianate style reminiscent of the building which had occupied the site prior to the construction of the precinct. Nowhere was this more obvious than in the design of the clock tower. *Photo Tim Fernandez.*

The Blackburn End stand at Ewood Park, rebuilt 1993-5, following Blackburn Rover's Return to top flight football and hailing a new era for the club. *Photo Tim Fernandez.*

be reflected in the Rovers, with them faring badly at times of economic strife and thriving in boom times. Founder members of the Football League in 1888, by a twist of fate they also became founder members of the new Premier League following promotion in 1992. The Rovers' return to the top flight was a spectacular one, finishing fourth, then runners up in only their first two seasons. By the close of the 1994/95 season, the championship was theirs. With Jack Walker's help, a new stadium and big named players came to the club but from 1995 onwards, the club seemed to lose their way, managing on several occasions to claw themselves out of the relegation zone, until 1999 when they suffered the ignominy of relegation. Another centuries old tradition is the annual fair which still rolls into the town each Easter. The blight of the authorities almost from time immemorial, this event too has faced its ups and downs with calls on several occasions for it to be stopped and having to undergo four changes in location after it was uprooted from the market square after 1964. In a hundred years the pace of the event has changed, though our Victorian contemporaries from the turn of the century would undoubtedly still recognise it as a place of fun and where nature makes way for the imagination. The Pot Fair trading element may have disappeared, but four of the rides of the 1999 event, 'the shaker', 'Musik Express', 'Dragon Coaster', and 'Snake Slide' are nineties, hi-tec versions of the turn of the century, 'Razzle Dazzle', 'Mont Blanc', 'Scenic Railway' and 'Helter Skelter' respectively.

The Royal Infirmary has also seen the century through, though after almost 150 years of caring for the people of Blackburn and District, is expected to close within ten years, with the Queen's Park Hospital, the former union workhouse, legacy of the poor laws of the nineteenth century taking over as the district's main hospital. Another of the town's traditions which has survived the century is that of brewing. The Lion Brewery of Matthew Brown, formerly Nuttall's, may have closed in 1990, but the name of Thwaites still lives on, as Blackburn's last remaining brewer edges towards it bicentennial celebrations in 2007, the last survivor in a town which boasted no less than eight independent breweries in 1900.

For Blackburn, the count-down to the millennium began in November 1998 with the starting of the 'millennium clock' on the town hall, activated by Blackburn motorcycle champion, Carl Fogerty with a second, placed on the Market Hall in Darwen, counting down the days, hours, minutes and seconds to 2000. As zero was reached the 31 December 1999, became 1 January 2000. the night sky over the town was white with the light of thousands of fireworks put up to welcome in this new year, the sound deafening and continuing at least half-an-hour, making this a momentous occasion. Although our parents, grandparents and great grandparents may have witnessed the turning of the century, nobody alive today, has experienced the changing of all the digits in the date. Yet, a thousand years after the start of the second millennium the Blakewater, the rivulet which gave the town its name, still flows through, though un-noticed these days, culverted beneath Salford, once the safe ford - the safe crossing point. Of all the institutions of Blackburn, only the Parish Church of St Mary can claim to have been there at the last millennium, having celebrated the 1,400th anniversary of its establishment back in 1996. The interim years have seen three buildings occupy the grounds of what is now Blackburn Cathedral now forming a centrepiece of the application for city status. But as for now, Blackburn is a noble town, with noble folk who are numbered with some of the greatest of them all. Both town and populace have endured the very worst of life over the last hundred years and yet in the face of such adversity have shown they

The River Blakewater, Witton Park, near to the point where it flows into the River Darwen, the Blakewater being the river from which the town derived its name. A very different view than that of Salford on page 135, which lies just two miles upstream. A thousand years ago this is how Salford might have looked to early travellers, near to the point where the settlement of Blackburn began to develop. *Photo Tim Fernandez.*

have had the strength to survive and survive they have. Now, as Blackburn moves towards the twenty-first century, it finds itself for once in a favourable position, with the possibility of leaving the twentieth century, on top of the world!

EVENTS 1990-1999.

1990
- Demolition of award winning deck access flats - Queen's Park.
- Poll Tax Protests, Blackburn's £1 a day, highest rate in Lancashire.
- Darwen owned horse, Rhinus come in third in Grand National.
- Milk race speeds through the town.
- Rover's fail to gain promotion in Division 2 play-offs
- Barbara Castle becomes Baroness Blackburn
- Closure of EH Booth's supermarket, ending a 106 year association with the town; catalogue company Argos take over the lease.
- Work begins on new Ice Arena, Audley.
- Facelift begins on town hall tower block.
- Closure of Lion Brewery.
- Demolition of the former Notre Dame Convent and girls' Grammar school.

1991
- Gulf War breaks out.
- Rovers appoint Kenny Dalglish as manager, following the sacking of Don Mackay.
- Visit of Princess Margaret to open care centre in Wellington St, St John.

- 14,000 women crowd into King George's Hall to see US Dance/strippers The Chippendales.
- Death of Rovers' Chairman, William Fox.
- Rovers end the year at the top of Division 2.
- Death of Blackburn-born author and fell walker, Alfred Wainwright.

1992

- Jack Straw returned as town's MP for fourth consecutive time, with increased majority of 6,033.
- Lord Taylor of Blackburn created freeman of the Borough.
- Blackburn fail for third time in bid to gain city status.
- Rovers' gain promotion to the new Premier League.
- Alan Shearer signs for Blackburn Rovers for £3million.
- Borough secures £35 million in grants through City Challenge

1993

- Go-ahead given for Rovers to build new super stadium at Ewood Park.
- Burst water main in King William Street floods shopping precinct.
- Closure of Waterfall Weaving Mill.
- Visit of the Prince of Wales.
- Rovers finish first season in Premier League in fourth position.

1994

- Passenger trains return on Clitheroe line.
- Facelift of markets complex begins closure of subways at Salford.
- Prime Minister, John Major takes part in Radio Lancashire phone-in.
- Rovers finish 1993/94 season as runners up.
- Unit 4 Cinema undergoes extensive alteration, emerging as the Apollo 5 Screen Cinema.
- Carl Fogerty wins Motorcycling World Championship.
- Rovers sign Chris Sutton for £5 million.
- Blackburn man scoops £17 million roll-over jackpot in the newly established National Lottery.
- 3Oth Anniversary of the opening of the new markets.

1995

- Town centre precinct undergoes facelift.
- Parade through the centre of town marks 50th Anniversary of VE Day.
- Blackburn Rovers win Premier League Championship for the first time in 82 years.
- Tree people take to the trees in Stanworth Woods near Feniscowles in protest of the building of the M65 motorway.
- Paul Wells captured by Kashmiri militants whilst on walking holiday in the region.
- Blackburn is nicknamed luckiest town in Britain after second person from the town scoops National Lottery Jackpot.
- £13 million extensions at Queen's Park Hospital opened by the Duchess of Gloucester.
- Kenny Dalglish resigns as manager of Blackburn Rovers, deputy, Ray Hartford takes the reigns.
- Service held at the cathedral in commemoration of the 50th anniversary of the VJ ending of the Second World War.
- Marks and Spencer open second sales floor.

1996

- Fund lauched to raise £700,00 to finance repairs to crumbling cathedral.
- Boulevard facelift begins.
- Sale of Alan Shearer to Newcastle for record breaking £17 million.
- Report suggest 40% of houses unfit to live in.

- Centenary of British cinema, plaques unveiled on Northgate on premises formerly the photographic shop of Sagar J Mitchell in recognition of his contribution to the development of the moving picture and on the former Lyceum Theatre, Market Street Lane, the first place in the town to exhibit moving pictures in Blackburn in 1896.
- Mayor launches 500 white balloons to mark the 500th day of the captivity of Paul Wells.
- Resignation of Ray Hartford as manager of Blackburn Rovers, Tony Parks acts as caretaker.

1997

- Jack Straw becomes the Home Secretary by retaining the Blackburn constituency seat with a staggering 14,000 majority, as the electoral landslide sweeps the Labour Party into power.
- Roy Hodgson becomes manager of Blackburn Rovers.
- Jack Straw opens the final section of the M65 motorway link.
- Demolition of the former Malvern Mill, (Co-op Discount Giant), Brothers Street.
- Death of Diana, Princess of Wales, (31 Aug), Televised funeral service brings town to a standstill, (6 Sept).
- The biggest selling single of all time, Elton John's 'Candle in the wind 1997, a tribute to the Princess of Wales, speedily manufactured at Philips.

1998

- Blackburn achieves unitary status, pulling away from county hall control as the Borough of Blackburn with Darwen, (1 April).
- TJ Hughes takes on a 20-year lease of the former Woolworth's store.
- Millennium clock on the town hall, activated by Carl Fogerty counting down the days to 2000.
- Go-ahead given for the building of a multiplex cinema behind Blackburn Railway Station.
- Brian Kidd takes control as manager of Blackburn Rovers following the sacking of Roy Hodgson.
- Approval of plan for new £5.5 million Railway Station.
- Announcement of Blackburn's intention to apply for city status.

1999

- Jack Straw removes bolt from platform clock on Blackburn Railway Station signalling the start of the £5.5 million revamp of the station.
- Woolworth return to the town.
- Plaque unveiled on Jubilee Street commemorating the centenary of the establishment of the town's electric tram network.
- In the first total eclipse seen in Britain since 1927, breaks in the clouds enable the people of Blackburn to observe 90% partiality (11 Aug).
- The Princess Royal visits to mark the rededication of the Cathedral lantern tower (30 Jun).
- First Asian Mayor of the Borough, Councillor Salas Kiani is selected.
- Visit of Prime Minister, Tony Blair.
- Kosovan Refugees arrive in the town.
- Visit of the former Pakistani Prime Minister, Benazir Bhutto.

2000

- Spectacular fireworks displays welcome in the landmark New Year (1 Jan).

INDEX